THE CHEMISTRY OF
SOME LIFE PROCESSES

Selected Topics in Modern Chemistry

SERIES EDITORS

Professor Harry H. Sisler
University of Florida
Gainesville, Florida

Professor Calvin A. VanderWerf
Hope College
Holland, Michigan

CHELDELIN AND NEWBURGH—*The Chemistry of Some Life Processes*
EYRING AND EYRING—*Modern Chemical Kinetics*
HILDEBRAND—*An Introduction to Molecular Kinetic Theory*
KIEFFER—*The Mole Concept in Chemistry*
MOELLER—*The Chemistry of the Lanthanides*
O'DRISCOLL—*The Nature and Chemistry of High Polymers*
OVERMAN—*Basic Concepts of Nuclear Chemistry*
ROCHOW—*Organometallic Chemistry*
RYSCHKEWITSCH—*Chemical Bonding and the Geometry of Molecules*
SISLER—*Chemistry in Non-Aqueous Solvents*
SISLER—*Electronic Structure, Properties, and the Periodic Law*
VANDERWERF—*Acids, Bases, and the Chemistry of the Covalent Bond*
VOLD AND VOLD—*Colloid Chemistry*

Series Editors Statement

Man's rapidly unfolding picture of the chemistry of life constitutes perhaps the most dramatic scientific saga of our time. The age-old riddles of growth and development, of reproduction and heredity, are on the verge of yielding to the concerted attack of biologist, chemist, physicist, and mathematician. Breakthroughs of monumental significance are in the offing.

In "The Chemistry of Some Life Processes," Drs. Cheldelin and Newburgh, writing from a rich background of teaching and research, have captured the excitement and majesty of the unfolding drama with no sacrifice of scientific or scholarly rigor. Here, in sound and solid terms, the beginning student catches the full breadth and sweep of the majestic story, as an introduction to more advanced study and as a springboard for an appreciation of the advances that lie ahead. In these pages chemistry comes to life for the student of chemistry and of biology alike.

HARRY H. SISLER
CALVIN A. VANDERWERF

THE CHEMISTRY OF
SOME LIFE PROCESSES

VERNON H. CHELDELIN

Dean, School of Science
Oregon State University

and

R. W. NEWBURGH

Assistant Director, Science Research Institute and
Professor of Chemistry
Oregon State University
Corvallis, Oregon

New York
REINHOLD PUBLISHING CORPORATION
Chapman & Hall, Ltd., London

PREFACE

You know that medicines when well used restore health to the sick: they will be well used when the doctor together with his understanding of their nature shall understand also what man is, what life is, and what constitution and health are.

LEONARDO DA VINCI

In essence this is the purpose of this book, to give the reader a small sample of what life is in chemical terms. To define all life in this way still eludes man, but our goal has been reached if your appetite has been whetted. Our hope is that you too might be stimulated to follow the path of the biochemist, the biophysicist, or the molecular biologist as he looks for answers within the living system.

Our debts are many to students, colleagues, and tutors alike, and one of us (R. W. Newburgh) particularly wants to acknowledge two, R. H. Burris and H. Herrmann. We are indebted to Mrs. Martha Brookes for the drawings.

Corvallis, Oregon   VERNON H. CHELDELIN
May, 1964   R. W. NEWBURGH

CONTENTS

chapter one ─────────────────────

LIFE'S BUILDING MATERIALS

EONS AGO, long before life's beginnings, the inanimate world had its inception. This world is often referred to as inorganic. Scientists long have understood what this embodies, even to understanding recently the minute particles of the atom. The atomic theory has long been a part of science. The atom has even been split to release forces more potent than Aladdin's genie.

When we reflect on the balance in our total knowledge of our natural surroundings, it is evident how little we know about the living compared to the nonliving. In a way this is a strange anomaly since all of us, scientist and nonscientist alike, must often ask questions intimately associated with man —a living creature. Such questions as: Who am I? How was I reproduced—like father, like son? How do I think? Why do I age? Why do I die? All of these are questions for which the biochemist seeks answers at the molecular level. Modern biochemistry strives for answers in the chemical processes of life. The development of the living organism is an orderly sequence of chemical events, triggered by chemical agents.

Biological chemistry (biochemistry for short) embraces not only chemistry, but also biology and physics. As a science it is only an infant, but a fascinating one. Thus far a simple description of life in physical and chemical terms has eluded students of this process; yet ultimate hope of success is confidently expected by many who observe closely the rapid progress that is being made.

Not only does biochemistry encompass a study of a basic understanding of life, but the student of this young daughter of chemistry seeks answers to the problems of disease. What is cancer? What causes heart disorders? Why do mental aberrations occur? These are but a few.

In the chapters to follow, we hope to introduce the reader to some of the fascination of biochemistry. One of the most important facets of this science is the relation of structure to function, that is, the attempt to show how a particular chemical structure is peculiarly related to a biological function.

Thus, in explaining the function of a nerve, we search for properties that would be inherent in the *kinds* of molecules or aggregations of molecules, that will impart electrical conductivity within an insulating sheath. When we attempt to explain muscle function, we search for one kind of molecule that is able instantly to generate the tiny bursts of energy that will power the whole organ and another kind that will be stretchable and contractible, as a rubber band. Nature is known to have been extremely ingenious in designing molecular types that possess the special ability to perform many unusual tasks. The unraveling of the mystery of the complex construction patterns continues to yield wondrous information to those who would seek answers.

Let us, then, begin our story by first assembling a suitable vocabulary. An understanding of the chemistry of living things calls for learning a formidable array of huge molecules, some of whose architectural characteristics are so unusual as to be almost unique and whose names present a barrier to easy learning. As there is no really simple way around this, the newcomer to the field must become familiar with a new language, that of the organic chemist, before he can wheel and deal and thrill in the nonfiction that describes the chemistry of life.

In spite of this, one need not be an orator or a poet in this foreign language, any more than is a peace corps emissary in a remote land. Despite the undeniably fundamental importance of organic chemistry to biology, we propose in these pages to vault over much of the detail, to try to glimpse a little earlier the exciting world of the living, mastering along the way only enough of organic architecture to develop an appreciation of its complexity.

Organic Compounds

The molecules that are found in living matter are very diverse, but nearly always contain the element *carbon*. Carbon has unusual bond-forming characteristics or valence properties. Most compounds are made up of a metal combined with one or more nonmetals. The nonmetals are strongly electronegative (electron-seeking), whereas the metals are electropositive (lose electrons easily). The resulting compounds usually exist as salts, with distinct ions being formed. Carbon, on the other hand, does little of this; it forms strictly covalent (sharing) bonds and displays a valence of four. This tendency to form covalent bonds is so pronounced that atoms of carbon frequently enter into combination with each other, forming long chains in this fashion:

$$-\overset{|}{\underset{|}{C}}-\overset{|}{\underset{|}{C}}-\overset{|}{\underset{|}{C}}-\overset{|}{\underset{|}{C}}-$$

Usually hydrogen is also combined with carbon; if the carbon skeleton above is fully combined with hydrogen the formula becomes butane. Compounds containing carbon and hydro-

$$H-\overset{\overset{\displaystyle H}{|}}{\underset{\underset{\displaystyle H}{|}}{C}}-\overset{\overset{\displaystyle H}{|}}{\underset{\underset{\displaystyle H}{|}}{C}}-\overset{\overset{\displaystyle H}{|}}{\underset{\underset{\displaystyle H}{|}}{C}}-\overset{\overset{\displaystyle H}{|}}{\underset{\underset{\displaystyle H}{|}}{C}}-H$$

Butane

gen (often other elements as well) are called *organic* compounds. This name is derived from the fact that these structures were discovered in living organisms. Although at first they were thought to occur only in living things, more recent discoveries in the nonliving world prohibit such an exclusive definition. Nevertheless, we recognize that all living matter (protoplasm) is made up of these carbon compounds, and the name *organic* is therefore still used to categorize compounds containing carbon and hydrogen, with or without other elements.

Because of the ability of carbon to combine with itself in endless ways, the number of organic structures possible is enormous. In 1940, a popular estimate of organic compounds then known to chemists was about 750,000; now 2,000,000 would be a better figure. Some notion of the diversity may be glimpsed by realizing that although all carbon atoms are alike, compounds containing carbon may be arranged in many combinations; using five carbon and twelve hydrogen atoms, one may have the three structures shown in Fig. 1-1.

Each of these structures is obviously different: the first is composed of an unbranched chain of carbon atoms. The second structure has one branch, and therefore one of its carbon atoms (number 3) is attached to three other carbon atoms and only one hydrogen. The third compound has two branches, and one of its carbon atoms (number 2) has no hydrogen connected to it at all. Although these three compounds are similar and are called *isomers*, since they all have the same molecular formula (C_5H_{12}), they are also all different: each has its own boiling point, its own melting point, and other individual physical and chemical properties.

The compounds just described are called *hydrocarbons* because they contain only carbon and hydrogen. Substances of this class are found in coal and petroleum, but the organic substances that compose most living things contain additional

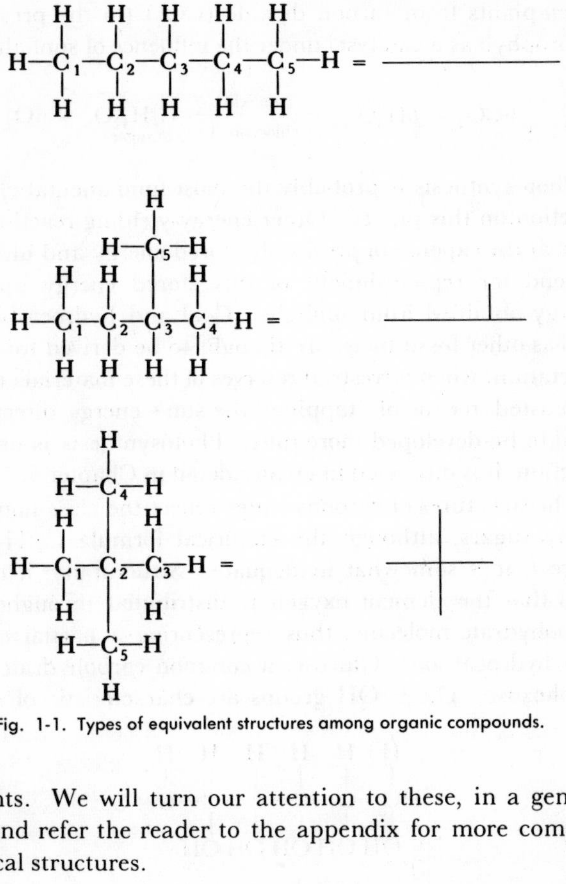

$$H-\underset{\underset{H}{|}}{\overset{\overset{H}{|}}{C_1}}-\underset{\underset{H}{|}}{\overset{\overset{H}{|}}{C_2}}-\underset{\underset{H}{|}}{\overset{\overset{H}{|}}{C_3}}-\underset{\underset{H}{|}}{\overset{\overset{H}{|}}{C_4}}-\underset{\underset{H}{|}}{\overset{\overset{H}{|}}{C_5}}-H \; = \; \underline{\hspace{3cm}}$$

$$H-\underset{\underset{H}{|}}{\overset{\overset{H}{|}}{C_1}}-\underset{\underset{H}{|}}{\overset{\overset{H}{|}}{C_2}}-\underset{\overset{\overset{H-C_5-H}{|}}{\underset{H}{|}}}{C_3}-\underset{\underset{H}{|}}{\overset{\overset{H}{|}}{C_4}}-H \; = \; \underline{\hspace{2cm}}|\underline{\hspace{2cm}}$$

$$H-\underset{\underset{\underset{\underset{\underset{H}{|}}{C_5}-H}{|}}{\underset{H}{|}}}{\overset{\overset{\overset{\overset{H-C_4-H}{|}}{H}}{|}}{C_1}}-\underset{}{C_2}-\underset{}{C_3}-H \; = \; +$$

Fig. 1-1. Types of equivalent structures among organic compounds.

elements. We will turn our attention to these, in a general way, and refer the reader to the appendix for more complex chemical structures.

Carbohydrates

Carbohydrates, which include sugars, starches, cellulose, and related materials, constitute the most abundant single class of organic compounds in nature. Their abundance is probably due to the fact that they are regularly formed by green plants from carbon dioxide (CO_2) (in the presence of chlorophyll as a catalyst) under the influence of sunlight.

$$6CO_2 + 6H_2O + \xrightarrow[\text{chlorophyll}]{\text{sunlight}} \underset{\text{(a sugar)}}{C_6H_{12}O_6} + 6O_2$$

Photosynthesis is probably the most fundamental chemical reaction on this planet. Other energy-yielding reactions proceed at the expense of previously stored energy and ultimately depend for replenishment of this stored energy upon the energy obtained from sunlight. Coal and hydrocarbons, as well as other fossil fuels, are thought to be derived from fossil vegetation; when terrestrial reserves of these materials become exhausted, means of "tapping" the sun's energy directly will need to be developed more fully. Photosynthesis is one such reaction; it is discussed in greater detail in Chapter 5.

The structures of carbohydrates reflect the class name: for many sugars, although the empirical formula $C_x(H_2O)_x$ is correct, it is somewhat inadequate. Structurally, it may be seen that the element oxygen is distributed throughout the carbohydrate molecule, thus representing a partial *oxidation* of a hydrocarbon. Glucose, a common carbohydrate, is an aldohexose. The —OH groups are characteristic of *alcohols*.

$$\begin{array}{ccccccc}
 & H & H & H & H & H & H \\
 & | & | & | & | & | & | \\
HC & -C & -C & -C & -C & -C & =O \\
 & | & | & | & | & | & \\
OH & OH & OH & OH & OH &
\end{array}$$

(an *aldo*hexose or aldose)

The —CHO group at the right end is characteristic of an *aldehyde*. When both types of groupings are present in the same molecule, the compound is called a sugar.

The carbon content of sugar molecules is extremely variable; a series of aldehyde–alcohol structures, in which the carbon atom chain is successively lengthened, appears in Table 1-1.

TABLE 1-1. Structures of a Series of Aldehyde Sugars

C_1 (no structure possible)

C_2 $H_2C-C=O$ a *di*ose (glycolaldehyde)
(with H above the C, OH below H_2C)

C_3 $H_2C-C-C=O$ a *tri*ose (glyceraldehyde)
(with H atoms above, OH OH below)

C_4 $H_2C-C-C-C=O$ a *tetr*ose
(with H H H above, OH OH OH below)

C_5 $H_2C-C-C-C-C=O$ a *pent*ose
(with H H H H above, OH OH OH OH below)

C_6 $H_2C-C-C-C-C-C=O$ a *hex*ose
(with H H H H H above, OH OH OH OH OH below)

C_7 $H_2C-C-C-C-C-C-C=O$ a *hept*ose
(with H H H H H H above, OH OH OH OH OH OH below)

C_8 $H_2C-C-C-C-C-C-C-C=O$ an *oct*ose
(with H H H H H H H above, OH OH OH OH OH OH OH below)

Branched chains may occur, giving rise to isomers; or the carbon doubly bonded to the oxygen may occur at an inner

$$H_2C-\overset{\displaystyle \overset{H}{|}}{C}-\overset{\displaystyle \overset{H}{|}}{C}-\overset{\displaystyle \overset{H}{|}}{C}-\overset{|}{\underset{O}{C}}-CH_2$$
$$\overset{|}{OH}\ \overset{|}{OH}\ \overset{|}{OH}\ \overset{|}{OH}\qquad \overset{|}{OH}$$

Fructose (a *keto*hexose or ketose)

position, as in the hexose, fructose. Thus, the number of possible isomers, all with the molecular formula $C_6H_{12}O_6$, is increased further.

Many still greater opportunities for structural variations among sugars result from the fact that virtually any of the foregoing compounds may exist in *polymeric* form, i.e., two or more chains may combine. Sugars consisting of two hexoses in such combination are illustrated by maltose. It will be seen

Maltose

that the molecular formula, $C_{12}H_{22}O_{11}$, is not quite equivalent to two molecules of isomeric glucose or other *mono*saccharides $(C_6H_{12}O_6 \times 2 = C_{12}H_{24}O_{12})$. Maltose differs from the formula for two glucoses by the removal of a molecule of water. The molecular formula might, however, be written $C_x(H_2O)_{x-1}$

and thus preserve the character of a "carbohydrate" (carbon plus water). Extension of this structure by a third hexose unit gives a *tri*saccharide $C_{18}H_{32}O_{16}$; four consecutive units form a *tetra*saccharide, and so on. The number of such polymers known is very large; examples occur in nature of individual molecules with two monosaccharide units up to more than a thousand; starch and cellulose, both polymers of hexose, are examples of polysaccharides. Still other compounds are polymers of pentoses, and so on.

Carbohydrates also exhibit *optical isomerism*; that is, if plane-polarized light is passed through a sugar solution, the plane of polarization is rotated.

Plane-polarized light is, as the name implies, light that travels in a single plane, as in Fig. 1-2a. It differs from light that emanates from a single point (Fig. 1-2b) in that the light in (a) has been "sliced" to

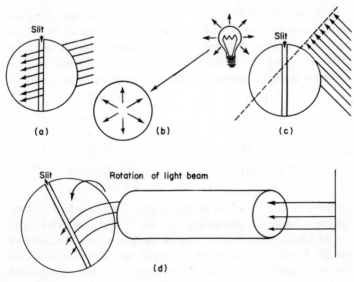

Fig. 1-2

permit the passage of only those rays that "line" up with the slit. Thus, even though the light rays in the polarized beam vibrate in waves perpendicular to the slit, the slit is only slightly wider than the amplitude of these waves; any light that approaches the slit at another angle, as in Fig. 1-2c, will be screened out. Plane-polarized light is obtained in practice by passing ordinary light through a Nicol prism. The special arrangement of the atoms in such a crystal provides the desired screen. A beam striking the prism along the dotted line shown in (c) would be screened out.

If a beam of polarized light is passed through a solution of an "optically active" compound dissolved in water, the plane or beam of the light is rotated (Fig. 1-2d). If the emergent beam shown in (d) enters another prism, it cannot pass through the orifice set as in (a). The prism must be rotated to coincide with the position shown in (d). The direction and the degree of rotation necessary are characteristic of the compound in question and are useful physical constants of the material, just as are melting and boiling points.

This rotation of the plane of polarization is explained as being caused by a "right-handedness" or left-handedness" of certain molecules. Molecules that can affect light in this way are those in which certain carbon atoms are attached to four different atoms or groups of atoms. An example is glyceral-

D-Glyceraldehyde   L-Glyceraldehyde

dehyde, in which carbon atom number 2 is attached to four different kinds of groupings: —H, —OH, —CHO, and —CH$_2$OH. (This is not true of carbon atom 1 since two valence bonds are connected to oxygen, nor of carbon 3, which has two bonds connected to hydrogen.) The compound D-glyceraldehyde rotates polarized light to the right; L-glyceraldehyde rotates polarized light to the left, *to the same degree.*

All chemical and physical properties of these two forms of glyceraldehyde are identical except for this equal but opposite rotation of the plane of plane-polarized light. These terms were originally derived from D = dextro (right) and L = levo (left). Although the significance of the terms has changed slightly during many years usage, they still refer to the right- or left-handedness of optically active molecules.

If a compound has four different groupings attached to a carbon atom it is called an *asymmetric* carbon atom. A compound with one asymmetric carbon atom has two isomers; a compound with two asymmetric carbons $2 \times 2 = 4$ or $2^2 = 4$, and so on. Careful inspection of sugar molecules reveals that they abound in carbon atoms having four different neighbors. Glucose, for example, has four such asymmetric carbon atoms (all except carbon atoms 1 and 6). Its spatial structure should be the one labeled D-glucose; the "left-handed" isomer or

$$
\begin{array}{cc}
\text{H} & \text{H} \\
| & | \\
\text{C}=\text{O} & \text{C}=\text{O} \\
| & | \\
\text{HCOH} & \text{HOCH} \\
| & | \\
\text{HOCH} & \text{HCOH} \\
| & | \\
\text{HCOH} & \text{HOCH} \\
| & | \\
\text{HCOH} & \text{HOCH} \\
| & | \\
\text{H}_2\text{COH} & \text{H}_2\text{COH} \\
\text{D-Glucose} & \text{L-Glucose}
\end{array}
$$

mirror image would be L-glucose. Since there are four asymmetric carbon atoms in glucose, one might confidently expect to find $2^4 = 16$ isomers of this aldohexose. This prediction of sixteen isomers has been verified experimentally; galactose, glucose, and mannose are but three of the sixteen, all naturally occurring and each with its own properties.

Pentoses, tetroses, and other monosaccharides all exist in

isomeric form; so do disaccharides and larger units. It is clear that a very large number of possible structures is soon easily reached. One feature that is especially interesting to consider is that living cells employ isomers in a selective manner; thus, when a given isomer is found to exist in tissues, its mirror-image compound (e.g., L-glucose) is often of no value biologically.

Amino Acids and Proteins

Some of the most important constituents of living matter are proteins. These compounds may be the structural elements of our cells or the molecules that catalyze the chemical reactions of the living system.

It is among these compounds that the greatest structural variations exist. Proteins as a class constitute lean meat, fish, or the cheese fraction of milk; in general they contain up to twenty "amino acids" that are often repeated many times over in each protein molecule. These twenty amino acids are all different in chemical structure, but they are also similar in that each amino acid possesses both an acid structure (—COOH) and a basic amino (—NH$_2$) group on adjacent carbon atoms:

$$
\begin{array}{c}
\text{H} \quad \text{O} \\
| \quad\ \ \| \\
\text{RC}\!-\!\text{COH} \\
| \\
\text{NH}_2
\end{array}
$$

where R represents any one of about twenty different hydrocarbon groups. Structures of several amino acids that are common to most proteins are shown in the appendix, page 113.

Most proteins are made up of virtually all the twenty amino acids, linked head-to-tail as shown in Fig. 1-3. The $-\overset{\displaystyle O}{\overset{\|}{C}}N-$ groups are called *peptide* bonds. The formation of each peptide

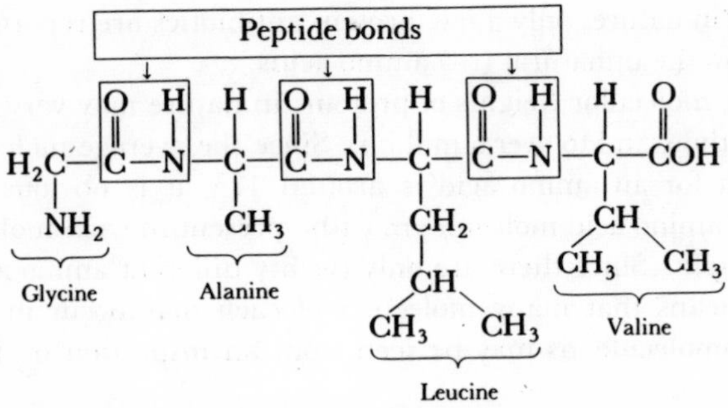

Fig. 1-3. Glycylalanylleucylvaline.

bond involves the elimination of water. This manner of linkage can proceed until all twenty amino acids are used several times over, and also in different sequences. It may be seen that the number of different protein structures possible is almost without limit.

Optical isomerism is also encountered among amino acids and proteins. Examination of the structure of alanine reveals an asymmetric carbon atom holding the amino group; thus two structures, D-alanine and L-alanine, are possible. Most other amino acids (except glycine) also possess one or more asymmetric carbon atoms, and may therefore exist in D- and L- forms. Yet, when normal protein chains are synthesized in the cell, the amino acid units nearly always occur in the L-configuration. Although D-amino acids may be synthesized readily in the organic chemist's laboratory, they are seldom

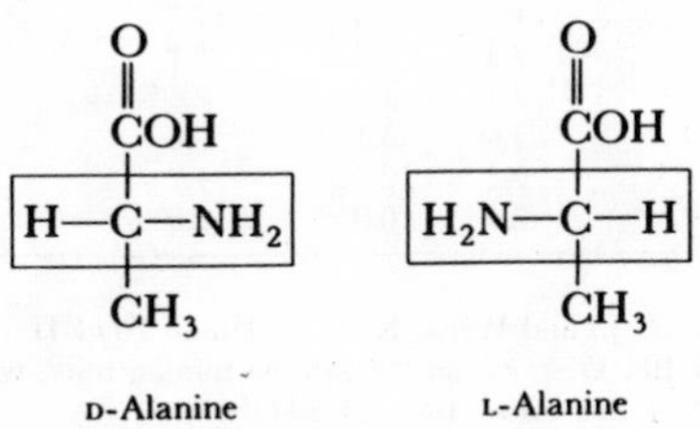

D-Alanine   L-Alanine

found in nature; only a few protein antibiotics are reported to contain the unnatural (D-) amino acids.

The molecular weights of proteins in nature may vary from a few thousand to over a million. Since the average molecular weight for an amino acid is around 125, it is obvious that many amino acid molecules must be present in each molecule of protein. Since there are only twenty different amino acids, this means that many molecules of each may occur in each macromolecule, as may be seen from an inspection of Table 1-2.

Eight of the common amino acids (isoleucine, leucine, lysine, methionine, phenylalanine, threonine, tryptophan, and valine) are essential in adult human diets; in addition,

TABLE 1-2.   Amino Acid Content of Some Animal and Plant Proteins (Percent)[a]

	Whole milk		Casein (cow)	Lactalbumin (cow)	β-Lactoglobulin (cow)	Hen's egg (whole)
	Human	Cow's				
[d]Arginine	5.0	3.5	4.2	3.1	2.9	6.7
[d]Histidine	2.7	2.7	3.0	1.8	1.7	2.4
[c]Lysine	7.2	8.0	8.2	9.7	11.9	6.9
[b]Tyrosine	5.1	4.9	6.3	3.2	4.0	4.1
[c]Tryptophan	1.9	1.3	1.5	1.8	2.3	1.6
[c]Phenylalanine	5.9	5.1	5.8	4.0	3.8	5.8
[b]Cystine	3.4	0.9	0.4	2.7	3.0	2.3
[c]Methionine	2.0	2.4	3.3	1.9	3.3	3.3
Serine		5.2	6.3	4.8	4.3	7.8
[c]Threonine	4.6	4.7	4.5	5.2	5.2	5.0
[c]Leucine	15.0	9.9	10.1	12.0	15.0	9.4
[c]Isoleucine	5.2	6.5	6.6	6.7	7.4	6.9
[c]Valine	5.5	6.7	7.4	5.3	5.8	7.4
Glutamic acid		21.7	23.6	17.7	19.8	12.6
Aspartic acid		7.5	6.5	11.1	11.7	8.2
Glycine		2.1	2.1	2.5	1.7	3.6
Alanine		3.6	3.1	7.0	6.8	
Proline		9.2	12.3	4.7	5.2	4.5
Hydroxyproline		0.0	0.0	0.0	0.0	

[a]Data from Block, R. J., and Weiss, K. W., "Amino Acid Handbook," Charles C Thomas, Springfield, Ill., 1956; except for data on human milk, which are from Block, R. J., and Bolling, D., *J. Am. Dietet. Assoc.* **20,** 69 (1944).

arginine and histidine are needed by growing rats. The other amino acids are synthesized by the organism. It is interesting to note how the contents of some of these compounds vary from one protein to another. Proteins such as gelatin (low in tryptophan) or zein (the chief protein in maize, low in tryptophan and lysine) are incomplete proteins with respect to their amino acid makeup and cannot sustain growth when fed as the only source of protein in a human or animal diet. Ovalbumin (egg white protein), on the other hand, is a complete protein; all of the amino acids that are essential in the diet are present in sufficient quantity to permit growth even if this compound is the sole source of edible protein.

There are only a few proteins that are as complete as oval-

TABLE 1-2 (continued)

Egg white	Muscle			Gelatin	Whole grain			Potato
	Fish	Fowl	Mammal		Corn meal	Whole wheat	Oatmeal	
5.9	6.6	6.7	6.6	7.8	4.4	4.3	6.9	5.3
2.5	2.9	2.0	2.8	0.8	2.4	1.8	2.2	1.8
6.4	10.1	7.7	8.5	4.8	2.7	2.5	4.4	5.3
4.3	2.4	2.7	3.1	0.6	4.6	3.6	3.9	2.5
1.8	0.9	1.0	1.1	0.01	0.7	1.2	1.2	1.1
6.0	3.8	4.1	4.5	2.0	4.5	4.4	4.8	5.1
2.6	1.2	1.0	1.4	0.1	1.6	3.3	1.2	1.2
4.0	2.8	2.4	2.5	0.9	1.8	1.2	1.5	2.1
7.3	3.5		5.1	3.4	4.4	3.8	3.7	2.6
4.7	4.5	4.0	4.6	1.7	4.1	3.9	3.7	3.7
9.0	7.9	8.2	8.0	3.5	12.7	6.9	7.2	6.2
6.4	5.2	4.2	4.7	1.4	4.0	4.4	4.9	5.1
7.8	5.5	4.1	5.5	2.7	5.3	4.5	5.3	5.9
12.8	12.0	17.0	14.6	7.8	18.4	31.4	14.3	7.4
7.6	8.6	10.5	8.0	4.9	12.3	3.8	4.1	9.8
3.7	5.4	5.7	5.0	15.7	3.5	3.4	3.6	1.9
	6.1		6.5	7.9	10.0	3.0	5.2	6.1
2.9	5.1		5.0	14.8	7.2	10.3	4.9	3.0
			4.7	13.3				

[b]Semiessential amino acids; i.e., cystine in good supply can spare about 90% of the methionine requirement; tyrosine can spare about half of the phenylalanine requirement.
[c]Essential amino acids in human diets.
[d]Additional amino acids essential in the diet of young rats.

bumin in their makeup, so that sound nutritional practice (as well as satisfaction of one's appetite) dictates that a variety of proteins be eaten regularly. This is especially important to millions of persons in Asia, Africa, and South America: many of these areas suffer from a scarcity of complete proteins, which are characteristically from animal sources; proteins of plant origin tend to be incomplete (low in lysine, low in methionine and cystine) and so should be varied in order to gain a maximum possible intake of marginal amino acids and thus prevent the onset of protein deficiency diseases. Inclusion of a little fish, for example, greatly improves the lysine intake in an all-cereal diet. Similar, although less spectacular, improvement may be noted in tryptophan intake when a little milk is added to an all-corn diet; even blending of corn with other cereals is of some help in an all-corn diet.

The details of protein structure are intricate, and the synthesis of these elaborate compounds is still incompletely understood. We shall see that information is available on this point, however, as we turn in Chapter 2 to a consideration of these and some related polymers, the nucleic acids.

Purine and Pyrimidine Bases; Nucleic Acids

One of the obvious and most important aspects of living systems is their ability to reproduce like kinds. A frog produces more frogs; an ant more ants. The compounds responsible for this hereditary process are the nucleic acids. Nucleic acids are the master that tells the living system what kind of proteins to make.

The gross characteristics of the nucleic acids are similar in some respects to those of the proteins. The nucleic acids are immense macromolecules, often having molecular weights of several million. They are also polymers of a very few building blocks replicated a thousand or more times in each macromolecule.

Although similar in gross characteristics, the variety of constituent units in a nucleic acid molecule is simpler than

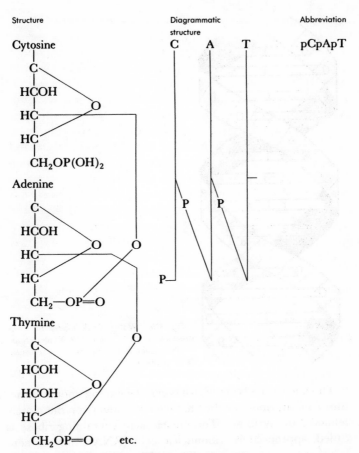

Fig. 1-4. Structure of nucleic acids.

that in a protein. Only two closely related sugars, inorganic phosphate ions, and four or five nitrogenous bases compose a typical nucleic acid. As in the proteins, the individuality of each nucleic acid is expressed through differences in combination and in changes in the sequences (or order) of the units in the macromolecular chain.

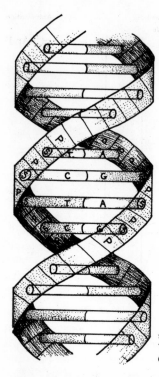

Fig. 1-5. Watson-Crick model of DNA structure. S = sugar; P = phosphate; T = thymine; A = adenine; C = cytosine; G = quanine.

The nucleic acids are of two types, depending upon whether they contain ribose as the characteristic sugar, or the closely related 2-deoxyribose. The nucleic acid containing ribose is called, appropriately, ribonucleic acid (RNA); the one containing deoxyribose, deoxyribonucleic acid (DNA). These two sugars, as well as the other constituent units of nucleic acids, are shown in the appendix, pages 114–115. Both RNA and DNA contain phosphate, in corresponding parts of the molecule. RNA contains, in addition, adenine, guanine, cytosine, and uracil; DNA is the same except for the replacement of uracil by thymine, which has a similar structure, as shown

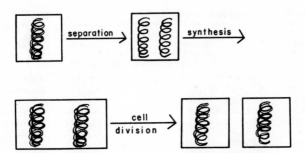

Fig. 1-6. Nucleic acid division accompanying cell division.

in the appendix, page 115. It follows from these statements that adenine, guanine, and cytosine may be found in combination with either sugar, but that uracil is associated only with ribose and thymine solely with deoxyribose. The combination of a base with the appropriate sugar is called a *nucleoside*.

Phosphate is attached to the sugar in nucleic acids as an ester. This new combination (base-sugar-phosphate) is referred to as a *nucleotide*. Both RNA and DNA consist of many nucleotides joined together by phosphate bridges between carbon atoms 3 and 5 of adjacent sugar molecules, as illustrated in the map in Fig. 1-4. The shorthand abbreviation used at the right in Fig. 1-4 is most advantageous when one needs to write the structure of a high molecular weight nucleic acid. Nucleic acid molecules occurring in nature are composed of many nucleotides in a single extended strand.

Scientists Watson and Crick, of Harvard and of Cambridge, England, respectively, shared the Nobel Prize in Medicine in 1962 for their demonstration of the three-dimensional structure of the DNA molecule. The structure, a model of which is shown in Fig. 1-5, consists of two strands of nucleotides coiled about one another in helical fashion. The bases are in the center and the phosphate and sugar molecules on the outside, as shown in Fig. 1-5.

TABLE 1-3.   Common Fatty Acids

No. of C atoms	Structure	Molecular formula	Name
A. Saturated (all C's except terminal C atom saturated with H)			
2	CH_3COOH	$C_2H_4O_2$	Acetic acid
4	$CH_3(CH_2)_2COOH$	$C_4H_8O_2$	Butyric acid
6	$CH_3(CH_2)_4COOH$	$C_6H_{12}O_2$	Caproic acid
8	$CH_3(CH_2)_6COOH$	$C_8H_{16}O_2$	Octanoic acid
10	$CH_3(CH_2)_8COOH$	$C_{10}H_{20}O_2$	Decanoic acid
12	$CH_3(CH_2)_{10}COOH$	$C_{12}H_{24}O_2$	Lauric acid
14	$CH_3(CH_2)_{12}COOH$	$C_{14}H_{28}O_2$	Myristic acid
16	$CH_3(CH_2)_{14}COOH$	$C_{16}H_{32}O_2$	Palmitic acid
18	$CH_3(CH_2)_{16}COOH$	$C_{18}H_{36}O_2$	Stearic acid
20	$CH_3(CH_2)_{18}COOH$	$C_{20}H_{40}O_2$	Arachidic acid
B. Unsaturated (having one or more pairs of double bonds (C=C) per molecule)			
18	$CH_3(CH_2)_7CH{=}CH(CH_2)_7COOH$	$C_{18}H_{34}O_2$	Oleic acid
18	$CH_3CH_2CH{=}CHCH_2CH{=}CH{-}CH_2CH{=}CH(CH_2)_7COOH$	$C_{18}H_{30}O_2$	Linolenic acid

Why was it necessary to propose two strands of DNA? When a cell divides to form two cells, the new cell formed is exactly like the previous cell. Thus, the DNA in this new cell is also identical. One explanation is that the original DNA is divided equally between the two cells as shown in Fig. 1-6.

Lipids (Fatty Substances)

The greaselike compounds, lipids, have been familiar to most of us from early childhood. It should surprise no one if their chief function in tissues were found to be one of lubrication. However, although the complete story of fat utilization is not yet known, it seems likely that these interesting compounds have other purposes besides merely serving as lubricants for tissues. Fats and oils, which are very similar in structure, are the prime high-energy fuels of nature, having more than twice as high a calorific value per unit weight as do carbohydrates or proteins. (Recently a possible connection between certain fats and the cardiovascular disease atherosclerosis has been suspected.)

The chief reason for the high fuel value of fats is that these compounds contain very little oxygen; they resemble hydrocarbons. Their structures vary; in general they are *esters*, which are made up of the alcohol glycerol combined with *fatty acids*. Fatty acids of natural occurrence are long-chain compounds, mostly even-numbered, which fall into the series shown in Table 1-3A. Most fatty acids in nature contain 16 to 26 carbon atoms per chain. In addition, a few are not fully saturated with hydrogen, having instead carbon-to-carbon double bonds in their structures, as shown in Table 1-3B.

Fats. These contain three molecules of fatty acid in combination with one molecule of glycerol, $C_3H_5(OH)_3$, as shown in Fig. 1-7. The structure given has three pairs of unsaturated (double) bonds per molecule, all of them contained in the linolenic residue. Fats containing more than one such pairs of double bonds per molecule are often oils at ordinary temperatures. A structure such as the one shown in Fig. 1-7 is said to have a reasonably high degree of unsaturation, or to be "polyunsaturated," hence prized by those who seek this type of compound for cooking purposes. Most cooking oils are high in unsaturated bonds (cottonseed oil is an exception).

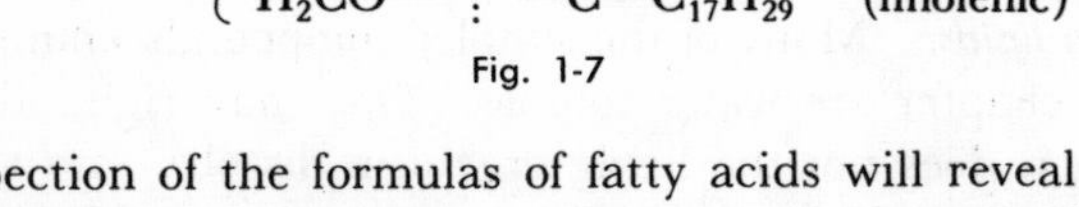

glycerol residue
H_2CO- $-C(=O)-C_{17}H_{35}$ (stearic)
$HCO-$ $-C(=O)-C_{15}H_{31}$ (palmitic)
H_2CO- $-C(=O)-C_{17}H_{29}$ (linolenic)

Fig. 1-7

Inspection of the formulas of fatty acids will reveal many opportunities for isomerism, especially when branched chain possibilities are included. In living tissue, however, these isomers are relatively few in number; natural fats seem to build up two carbon atoms at a time in straight chains, so

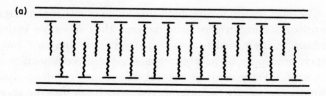

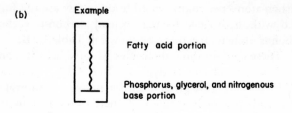

Fig. 1-8. Schematic drawing of a membrane.

that only a relatively small number of isomers exist. The fats, in contrast to the carbohydrates, occur in nature in far fewer variations than might be expected.

Other lipids. Many of the simpler compounds enumerated in this chapter are water soluble. One may rightfully ask, why then does not the living organism dissolve into a small (or large) droplet? Part of the answer is provided by the enormity of the polymeric molecules present; even though the constituent monomeric units are soluble, such molecular aggregates as starches, cellulose, proteins and nucleic acids are nearly insoluble in water at ordinary temperatures, due to their molecular size.

Lipids are also partially responsible for the low water-solubility of tissues. They (the lipids) are almost insoluble in water, but are quite soluble in organic solvents that are often referred to as "fat solvents," principally acetone, alcohol, ether, petroleum ether, chloroform, and carbon tetrachloride. Lipids, which are important constituents of all membranes, exist in combination with proteins. Most membranes viewed with an electron microscope consist of a layer of lipid-type molecules sandwiched between two protein layers (see Fig. 1-8).

In addition to the triglycerides discussed under fats, other distinct groups of lipids are also found in biological materials. One, related to the triglycerides, is composed of a glycerol residue esterified with a single molecule of fatty acid (a monoglyceride) or with two molecules of fatty acid (a diglyceride). Another important group of lipids is known as the *phospholipids;* a typical phospholipid compound contains phosphate, two fatty acid residues, and a nitrogenous base. The phospholipids are primary constituents of tissue membranes. Although they are structurally related to fats and oils, they are also often regarded as being derived from α-glycerophosphoric acid.

$$
\begin{array}{l}
CH_2OH \\
\mid \\
HCOH \qquad\quad O \\
\mid \qquad\qquad\quad \parallel \\
CH_2\!-\!O\!-\!P\!-\!OH \\
\qquad\qquad\quad \mid \\
\qquad\qquad\quad OH
\end{array}
$$

α-Glycerophosphoric acid

Steroids.   Another group of lipids, the *steroids*, are derivatives of phenanthrene, a hydrocarbon. (Ring structures such as the structure for phenanthrene are abbreviated, to imply the presence of a C atom at each corner of a ring. H atoms

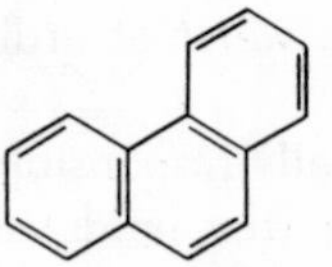

Phenanthrene

should be added at each location until the valence number reaches four.)

The major member of the steroid group is cholesterol, a sterol isolated in 1775 from gallstones. It has a complex structure, as shown. Cholesterol has been studied extensively

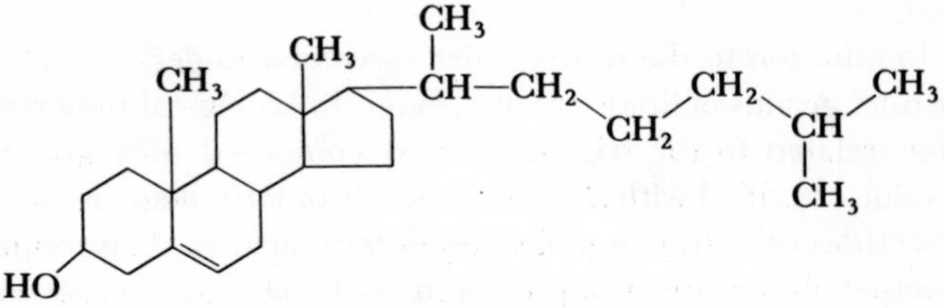

Cholesterol

due to its relation to the heart disease, atherosclerosis. In this disease, cholesterol is deposited on the inner walls of arteries. This eventually restricts the flow of blood, resulting in death. One of the prevailing arguments for minimizing the amount of animal fats in the diet is that these are converted to cholesterol; excess cholesterol accumulates and is deposited on the arterial walls.

Various other steroids have different uses, especially in the bodies of higher animals. Prominent among these are some of the vitamins and hormones. These will be discussed next.

Hormones and Vitamins

Before closing out the inventory of life's building materials, we need to include two additional groups of compounds, both of which probably participate in catalytic functions in the

Estrone
(an estrogen)

Testosterone
(an androgen)

living cell. Certainly this is true of most of the vitamins; we are not yet so sure about the hormones.

The first noteworthy group of hormones are steroids. Hormones of this chemical type include compounds that are generated in the cerebral cortex, the pituitary gland, and the adrenal gland; these regulate growth processes as well as the overall balance between water and various electrolytes (salts) in human and animal systems. Others, called androgens and estrogens, are responsible for secondary sex characteristics, male and female, respectively. The estrogens arise in the ovaries, androgens chiefly in the testes. Their structures are quite similar. Inspection of their structures discloses a chief difference between them to be the presence of an extra methyl group in testosterone. We may therefore differentiate here between the sexes: one methyl group!

Still other hormones are proteins; some are smaller peptides, while others have miscellaneous structures. Indeed, neither hormones nor vitamins bear much chemical resemblance to one another. This stands in contrast to other groups of cellular constituents, such as the carbohydrates, which are all of one chemical type. Both the vitamins and hormones are classified together largely because they may have the common biological property of serving as parts of biocatalyst systems.

The vitamins are needed in the diet in minute amounts, in contrast to the hormones, which are regularly synthesized

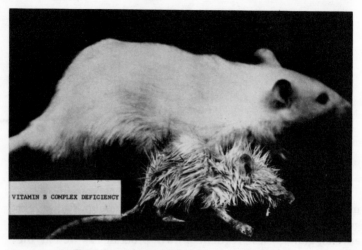

Fig. 1-9. Multiple vitamin deficiency in the albino rat.
These two animals are littermates, age approximately 2 months.   Several vitamins have been withheld from the diet of the animal in the foreground for a period of 5 weeks. (Courtesy of S.M.A. Corporation)

in our bodies. The common vitamins, together with some observations regarding their physiological and biochemical functions are listed in the appendix, page 116. Fig. 1-9 illustrates the importance of these biocatalysts: if several vitamins are simultaneously withheld from the diet of a young rat, a miserable specimen, such as that pictured in the foreground, results.

The chemical substances described in this chapter constitute most of life's important building materials. In size they vary from the small to the very large. Separately, they serve little purpose in the area of the living, but meshed into interrelated parts they form the essence of life. In Chapter 2, we will direct further attention to the two classes of compounds, proteins and nucleic acids, that establish in a real sense the *thread of life*.

THE THREAD OF LIFE

CURIOSITY killed the cat! Fortunately, this popular saying is not applicable to the biochemist. Inquisitiveness into the essence of nature not only furthers our knowledge of ourselves and our surroundings, but often leads to answers permitting maximal survival. Man pursues this to the ultimate in an attempt to learn how life began and then perpetuated itself. Not only does this study provide a scientific basis for the origin of a species, but it also helps to understand each new conception. Each living organism begins life as a single cell that contains all the information necessary to develop into a whole being fabricated exactly like the one that preceeded it. This is the thread of life. Present information reveals that two chemical constituents of living matter are intimately associated with this process—the continuity of life. These are proteins and nucleic acids.

Proteins

Our bodies consist of many proteins, each one differing in some way to permit it to participate in a particular chemical reaction. One protein may be an enzyme, another a molecule in skin or hair, still another a hormone. Each has a particular role in the living organism. In other words, it is specific in its function. Specificity then, is the most important aspect of proteins. What imparts this specificity? In recent years biochemists have shown that this is largely the result of the sequence of the amino acids: that is, the order in which they occur in a protein.

Let us look at a simple hypothetical example to see how changes in the sequence may lead to formation of different proteins. If we assume that a protein contains three different amino acids, A, B, and C joined by two peptide bonds (—), then by changing the order, we can write six different proteins: (1) A—B—C, (2) A—C—B, (3) B—A—C, (4) B—C—A, (5) C—A—B, and (6) C—B—A. The sequence is different in each instance. Mathematically we can interpret this as 3 factorial (3!) (3 × 2 × 1 = 6). If proteins consisted of only one unit each of twenty amino acids, we may have factorial 20 (20!) or some two billion billions (2 × 10^{18}) different proteins as the result of only a change in the order of the amino acids. Actually, a protein with only twenty amino acids would be small (approx. 2500 molecular weight). This is a tiny figure since most known proteins have a molecular weight nearer 100,000, some more than 1,000,000. We can illustrate our sequence of three amino acids somewhat differently to show that A—B—C and C—B—A are really different.

Let

$$A = NH_2—\overset{\overset{\displaystyle O}{|}}{\underset{\underset{\displaystyle H}{|}}{C}}—COOH \qquad B = NH_2—\overset{\overset{\displaystyle \triangle}{|}}{\underset{\underset{\displaystyle H}{|}}{C}}—COOH$$

$$C = NH_2—\overset{\overset{\displaystyle \square}{|}}{\underset{\underset{\displaystyle H}{|}}{C}}—COOH$$

where the R groups are illustrated by different symbols indicating the organic radicals of different amino acids.

The A—B—C would be

$$NH_2-\underset{\underset{H}{|}}{\overset{\overset{\bigcirc}{|}}{C}}-\overset{\overset{O}{\|}}{C}-NH-\underset{\underset{H}{|}}{\overset{\overset{\triangle}{|}}{C}}-\overset{\overset{O}{\|}}{C}-NH-\underset{\underset{H}{|}}{\overset{\overset{\square}{|}}{C}}-COOH$$

and CBA

$$NH_2-\underset{\underset{H}{|}}{\overset{\overset{\square}{|}}{C}}-\overset{\overset{O}{\|}}{C}-NH-\underset{\underset{H}{|}}{\overset{\overset{\triangle}{|}}{C}}-\overset{\overset{O}{\|}}{C}-NH-\overset{\overset{\bigcirc}{|}}{C}-COOH$$

Note that in A—B—C the amino (NH_2) group of A is free and the carboxyl (COOH) group of C is free; while in C—B—A, the amino group of C is free and the carboxyl of A is free.

One of the fascinating problems of modern biochemistry has been the decoding of sequences of amino acids in proteins. In a brilliant study, Dr. Sanger of Cambridge University, England, determined the sequence existing in the protein hormone, insulin. The results are shown in Fig. 2-1.

We may ask, how does one determine this order? Suppose the individual amino acid units in a protein are represented by ●, as done in Fig. 2-2. Immediately we note something peculiar about amino acids number 1 and 2. Number 1 has a free amino group and number 2 a free carboxyl group. Proteins can be hydrolyzed (that is, the peptide bonds can be broken to release amino acids) in a strongly acid environment. If we hydrolyzed an unmarked protein, this would tell us what amino acids were present, but would tell nothing about the sequence. On the other hand, if we used a marker to label

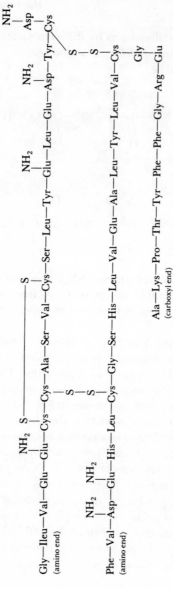

Fig. 2-1. Amino acid sequence in insulin.

The letters are abbreviations for the common amino acids, some of which are listed in Fig. 1-2. Additional compounds are:
Asp—NH₂ = asparagine (a relative of aspartic acid), $H_2NOCCH_2CHNH_2COOH$; glu = glutamine, the corresponding relative of glutamic acid, $H_2NOCCH_2CH_2CHNH_2COOH$.

either the free amino (1) or carboxyl group (2) prior to hydrolysis, then hydrolysis of the protein and separation of the amino acids would yield one marked amino acid. We would know its position in the sequence. Dinitrofluorobenzene is such a marker.

Dinitrofluorobenzene reacts with a free amino group to yield a dinitrophenyl amino acid. If we then hydrolyze the protein, we will obtain all of the amino acids, but one of them

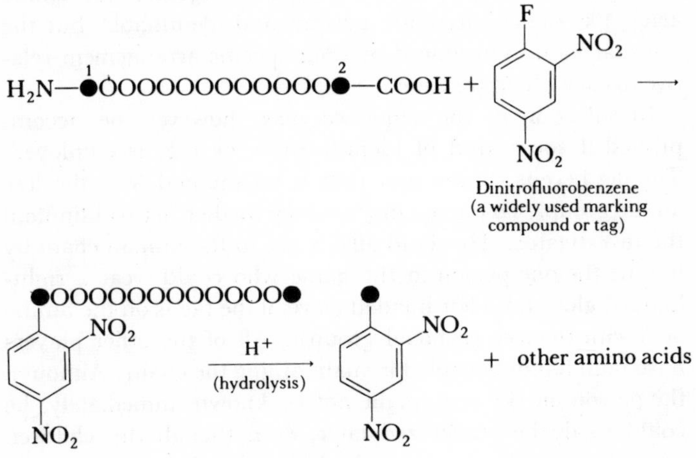

Dinitrofluorobenzene
(a widely used marking
compound or tag)

Fig. 2-2

will be different from the others. It is distinct from the others since its amino group is substituted by the dinitrophenyl group. By using chromatographic procedures, we can separate and identify this particular amino acid. Determination of the sequence of the other amino acids is more complex, but essentially consists of a repetition of this same method. Rather than hydrolyzing the protein completely into its constituent amino acids, one partially hydrolyzes it into small peptides and by comparisons eventually determines the whole sequence.

The significance of the sequence of amino acids in a long polypeptide chain may be compared to that of a sequence of school children joined hand to hand, in a playground game such as "Red Rover." When they have reconvened in the classroom after the game, the erstwhile sequence is lost, much the same as the sequence of amino acids is lost when the amino acids are hydrolyzed by chemical agents: the amino acids, like the children, are present and identifiable, but the unusual features produced by their specific arrangement relative to each other are gone.

Recollection of the sequence may, however, be accomplished if some kind of identification, or tag, is employed. The tag here is on the unit that is on the end with the free amino group. To pursue our analogy further, let us blindfold the investigator. He could affix a tag to the human chain by finding the one person in the game who could wear a right-handed glove (or a left-handed glove, if the tag is on the amino acid with the free carboxyl group). All of the other players have both hands occupied in maintaining the chain. Although the person on the end might not be known immediately, he could easily be recognized later, even though the children were dismissed (the protein hydrolyzed); the child wearing the glove is recognized by his tag, and his position is also known: he stood at the (free amino) end of the chain. Dinitrofluorobenzene is the tag used for this purpose.

We recognize that a new game for simple folk could be concocted by reforming the line in a different sequence, handing the glove to a new person on the end, and identifying him in turn. But the protein molecules are not so fickle; our best evidence suggests that when they reform, they do so in the same sequence as before. (The master directive force, or template, that causes the amino acids to "count off" and find their correct positions, will be discussed later.) However, the entire operation described has only identified the player at the end of the line; the sequence of the remaining members would remain a mystery, if it were not for the fact that methods also exist for the partial hydrolysis of proteins. A chain of 25 amino acid units can be broken up into shorter chains containing three or four or up to eight or ten amino acids. Each of these smaller chains has a new end unit (generated in the hydrolysis reaction), which can now engage the reagent dinitrofluorobenzene, and thus the end units of the subchains are recognized; further degradations reveal additional actors (always at the end of their particular fragment of a previously held longer chain). The detective game continues until all the pieces are fitted together and the sequence of amino acids in the original protein or polypeptide is deduced. This is essentially what Sanger and his associates did. (The task required several years, and one of the consequences was his winning the Nobel Prize in Chemistry for 1958.)

The proteins, which are huge molecules, occupy three dimensions in space; many take the shape of a screw, or helix. The structure is idealized in Fig. 2-3a; Fig. 2-3b and c shows a scale model of the same type (an ascending helix, rotating like a winding staircase), with 3.7 amino acid residues per turn, which has been developed to describe the structure of the keratin molecule, as well as certain muscle proteins. This structure, plus another helix more loosely bound with 5.1 residues per turn (Fig. 2-3c) was described by Professor Linus Pauling and his co-workers at the California Institute of Technology. The values were set to conform to data obtained from X-ray analyses of these proteins. It should be stressed that the pictures in Fig. 2-3 are not photographs of actual protein molecules, but rather are diagrams of models. They are scale models, however, that are constructed from the

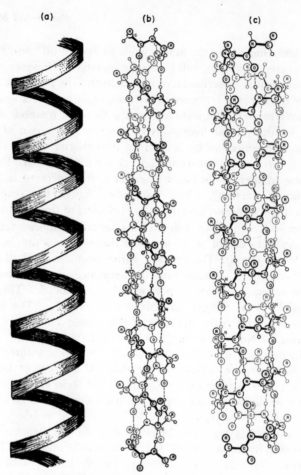

Fig. 2-3. Helical shape of protein molecules.

(a) Artist's drawing of generalized helical shape. (b) α-helix with 3.7 residues per turn. (c) Similar structure with 5.1 residues per turn.

The figures shown represent "left-handed" helices composed of D-amino acid residues; they are the equivalent of a "right-handed" helix of L-amino acid residues. Translation along the axis of the helix in the 3.7-residue model is 1.47 Å, whereas that in the 5.1-residue is 0.99 Å, respectively. The hydrogen bonds (shown as dotted lines) that connect several of the —C≡O and —NH— groups are calculated to be 2.7 to 2.8 Å in length.

X-ray data; the indirect pictures obtained are regarded with great confidence by physical scientists. The ingenious patterns worked out in Fig. 2-3 earned Pauling the Nobel Prize in Chemistry in 1954.

More recently, examination of X-ray photographs has been improved by Professors Kendrew and Perutz of Cambridge, England, to permit resolution (quantitative detection) to 2 Å. distance. (The average carbon-carbon bond length is about 1.5 Å.) Having thus "sharpened their spectacles," they observed that the protein myoglobin (a muscle pigment) exists largely in a folded helical pattern, as shown in Fig. 2-4, similar to the 3.7 residue helix that Pauling had previously calculated. For their work, Kendrew and Perutz won the Nobel Prize in Chemistry in 1962.

Enzymes. Many proteins have been studied to date; specificity has been determined, and invariably different sequences have been found. We belive that it is this sequence which gives specificity to proteins and in turn specificity to life. Not only do we mean specificity regarding the difference between nerve and heart cells, for example, but also specificity among a vital group of proteins called enzymes. Some scientists describe life as a system of integrated cooperating enzyme reactions.

We hear much about enzymes; just what are they, and how do they function? Chemically, we can state categorically that all enzymes are proteins. When the protein casein is chemically hydrolyzed to its constituent amino acids (this occurs naturally whenever milk is drunk), we must add 10 times its weight of concentrated mineral acid and boil the mixture for 20 hr. If we use in place of mineral acids the lining of the stomach of a recently slaughtered animal, the casein will be hydrolyzed to its amino acids in a few hours at body temperature because of the enzyme reactions present. When the enzyme that hydrolyzes casein is purified, it will hydrolyze some 10,000 times its own weight of casein. This is why we often hear enzymes described as biological catalysts. A little does a great deal and goes a long way.

The biochemist is interested in knowing what actually

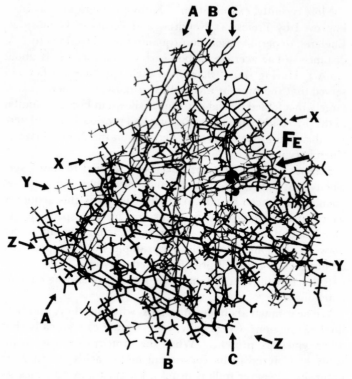

Fig. 2-4. Three-dimensional structure of myoglobin.

Kendrew, Perutz, and their colleagues have examined X-ray patterns of myoglobin and have found the structure to be represented by the diagram above. Careful inspection of this 150-amino acid polypeptide chain reveals the presence of (a) a heme unit (contains iron) at Fe and (b) several helical sections such as those running in the direction of the vertical arrows A, B, C and the horizontal arrows, X, Y, Z. It has been estimated that a folded helical structure accounts for about 75% of the amino acids in the diagram. (From J. C. Kendrew, *Sci. Am.* **205**, No. 6, 96 (1962).)

causes this hydrolysis under so mild conditions. He usually first attempts to isolate the enzyme, in a fashion similar to that shown in Fig. 2-5. This is an enzyme purification. How do we know we have purified the enzyme? To learn this we must determine two criteria. First we need to know the total activity—that is, the amount of protein that our enzyme will hydrolyze to the constituent amino acids in a given time. Next, we want to learn what portion of the total protein from the source material (stomach) is composed of the enzyme in question. We also know that a certain amount of total activity

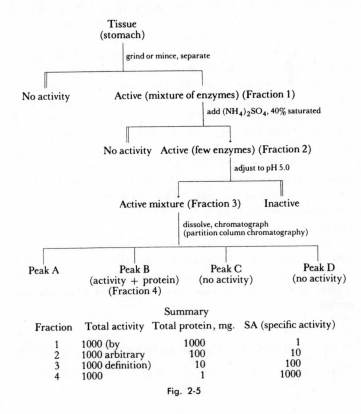

Summary

Fraction	Total activity	Total protein, mg.	SA (specific activity)
1	1000 (by	1000	1
2	1000 arbitrary	100	10
3	1000 definition)	10	100
4	1000	1	1000

Fig. 2-5

may be ascribed to this enzyme. Of course, the starting material or source, i.e., the stomach, is a mixture of many enzymes or proteins. Our task is to remove these unwanted proteins from the enzyme. Thus, it is evident that if we divide the activity by the amount of protein present we obtain a figure called specific activity. The higher the specific activity the greater is the quantity of the desired enzyme in the total proteins.

By analogy let us suppose that we have a mixture of 30 marbles of different colors, 10 red, 15 blue, and 5 green. This means that the red marbles have an "activity" (frequency) of 10 and represent 10/30 of all the marbles. Here the color of the marbles permits visual separation. In a similar sense, various physical and chemical characteristics permit analytical instruments to "see" different kinds of proteins, although perhaps not as easily. If we now eliminate the green marbles, the red marbles represent 10/25 of the total, that is, we have concentrated them from 10/30 (= 33%) to 10/25 (= 40%). If we next eliminate the blue marbles, only the red ones remain; these now represent 10/10 or 100% of the total marbles that are left. In other words, these treatments have successively separated the red marbles from the others, or conversely, have removed the unwanted ones. This is the same as removing extraneous proteins from a desired enzyme until it is the only one remaining.

Once the enzyme is purified we can determine the materials with which it reacts. Some enzymes attack only proteins, and are called proteolytic (protein-dissolving) enzymes, or proteases. With such enzymes, the following type of reaction occurs:

$$\underset{\underset{NH_2}{|}}{RCHC}\overset{\overset{O}{\|}}{}\underset{\underset{R}{|}}{\overset{\overset{H}{|}}{N}CHCOOH} + H_2O \rightarrow \underset{\underset{NH_2}{|}}{RCHCOOH} + \underset{\underset{R}{|}}{H_2NCHCOOH}$$

The hydrolysis does *not* proceed with other types of bonds, for example, $RCHCOOCH_2CH_3$. Thus, this particular enzyme exhibits specificity since it reacts only with specific compounds. Some enzymes react only with one chemical compound, others with a group of compounds with similar structures, whereas a few may permit action on a broader variety of materials. Biochemists believe that for nearly every chemical reaction taking place in a living cell, there is a separate enzyme.

We may now list three characteristics of an enzyme: (1) Chemically, they are all proteins. (2) They act catalytically. (3). They are specific for particular compounds. This specificity is due to their own amino acid sequences.

In an enzymic reaction we refer to the compound that reacts with the enzyme as the substrate. In the reaction a combination occurs between the substrate (S) ("subject molecule") and the enzyme (E) as follows:

$$E + S \rightleftharpoons ES \rightleftharpoons E + \text{products}$$

Without enzymes, biochemical processes would be too slow to carry on life. In the enzyme reaction just cited, the enzyme was not altered chemically. This makes it similar to other catalysts in chemical reactions where the catalysts partake in the reactions but are not themselves used up. The proteolytic enzyme also breaks down proteins much faster than does mineral acid. Therefore, one function of the enzyme is to increase the rate of the reaction. As an example, the chemical reaction:

$$H_2CO_3 \rightarrow CO_2 + H_2O$$

is very rapid. When a bottle of carbonated soda is opened, we appreciate how rapidly this reaction occurs. The same reaction occurs in the lungs when we generate carbon dioxide. Yet, if one calculates the rate of the chemical reaction given and also the rate at which we respire carbon dioxide, it is realized that the uncatalyzed reaction is not rapid enough to sustain life. Our bodies have an enzyme called carbonic anhydrase, which is able to hasten this action.

Rate (hypothetical), CO_2/min.

Chemical

$$H_2CO_3 \rightarrow CO_2 + H_2O \qquad\qquad 1$$

Biological

$$H_2CO_3 + E \rightarrow [H_2CO_3{-}E]\rightarrow$$
$$CO_2 + H_2O + E \qquad\qquad 2$$

Next we may ask, how does this occur? By the end of the 19th century chemists had already understood that a molecule must obtain extra energy from another molecule before it can react. This may happen when one molecule collides with another. The molecules with extra energy are said to be "activated" (indicated by an asterisk):

$$S \rightarrow S^* \rightarrow \text{products}$$

How might an enzyme fit into this scheme? For the decomposition of carbonate to occur, a certain activation energy is necessary. This is a kind of wall or barrier to activity. If this barrier is lowered the reaction will proceed more easily since it has a lower wall to breach. This may be seen when the enzyme catalase acts by lowering the activation energy for the decomposition of hydrogen peroxide (Fig. 2.6 illustrates this qualitatively.)

E_a, cal./mole

1. $H_2O_2 \xrightarrow{\text{(no catalyst)}} H_2O + \frac{1}{2}O_2$ 18,000

2. $H_2O_2 + Fe \longrightarrow H_2O + \frac{1}{2}O_2$ 13,000

3. $H_2O_2 + \text{catalase} \rightarrow H_2O + \frac{1}{2}O_2$ 5,000

Nucleic Acids

For each chemical reaction occurring in a living organism there is a different enzyme. This is an example of the spe-

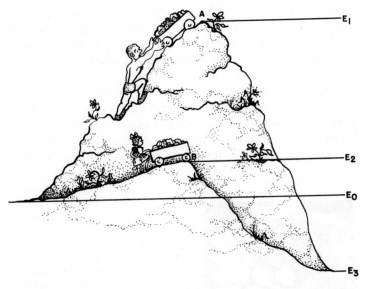

Fig. 2-6. Mechanism of enzyme action in a spontaneous, energy-yielding (exergonic) reaction.

All reactions, whether catalyzed or not, require some activation energy to initiate the reaction. An analogy is obtained in this figure: On the upper hill (an uncatalyzed reaction), the wagon must be raised to the top of the hill to point A, with energy E_1, in order to start spontaneous motion downhill and form a product having energy content E_3. The total net energy yield in the reaction is $E_0 - E_3$, since the energy of activation, $E_1 - E_0$, had to be supplied before it could again be realized in the (spontaneous) reaction.

When an enzyme is present, as on the lower hill, it provides a detour through passes around the mountain, still at a partially increased energy level B (energy E_2) but lower than the hilltop plane needed in A in the absence of enzymes. The net energy yield from the reaction is still $E_0 - E_3$; thus the total yield of product is unchanged, although the speed of the reaction is greatly increased in the presence of enzymes because of the lower activation energy needed ($E_1 - E_2$).

cificity of a protein. A question that logically arises is, what mechanism controls this specificity? We know that with each new generation in a species of organisms, a new set of enzymes is synthesized, whose members are essentially identical to those in the organism's ancestors.

One of the clues to the solution of the problem of specificity arose as a result of studies by Fraenkel-Conrat at the University of California on the tobacco mosaic virus (Fig. 2-7). A virus is a parasitic organism, able to reproduce itself in a host cell (in this discussion the tobacco plant). Viruses are con-

Fig. 2-7.   Model of tobacco mosaic virus.

Investigators at the University of California, Berkeley, and at Tübingen, Germany, have found that the immense protein portion of the molecule (molecular weight about 50 million) is in reality made up of a polypeptide unit repeated 150 times, with the usual twenty amino acids occurring throughout each unit. The units are, in turn, repeated 2200 times.   The picture that emerges resembles a huge cluster of grapes with each grape representing the 150-member unit. The central core is the nucleic acid, but wound like a coiled spring rather than existing as a grape stem.   Description of the virus reveals to the biochemist that the molecule, despite its enormous size, is far simpler than might have been supposed. For one thing, the repetition of the same sequence 2200 times reduces the complexity greatly; the fact that the RNA rather than the protein portion carries the infectivity, reduces the complexity still further, though this core of nucleic acid (molecular weight 2–3 million) is more complicated than most other known chemical structures. (Courtesy of Dr. H. Fraenkel-Conrat)

venient tools to use in studies of specificity since they consist of only a protein, together with a nucleic acid that is present in the tobacco mosaic virus. The kind of nucleic acid present is RNA (ribonucleic acid). The virus consists of only a core of RNA and a protein coat in a ratio of 5 parts nucleic acid to 95 parts protein. Fraenkel-Conrat observed a most interesting phenomenon concerning the relation of this RNA to the protein coat. A diagram of the relationships observed is given in Fig. 2-8.

As can be seen from the diagram, RNA controlled the kind of protein to be synthesized. Thus, some sort of code exists in RNA that can determine how amino acids will be arranged in a particular protein; to return to the analogy of the "Red Rover" game, RNA is the controller that arranges the sequence of the children in the lineup. When we look at a more

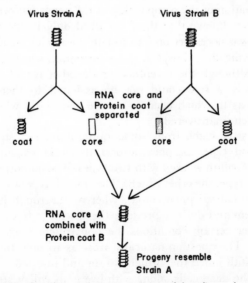

Fig. 2-8. Role of nucleic acids in transmission of hereditary characteristics.
▭ RNA; ⦿⦿⦿⦿⦿ Protein

complex organism such as ourselves, the situation becomes even more involved.

Biologists in years past had shown that various characteristics were passed down by heredity, and they had come to believe that a separate gene existed for every trait. More recently they have shown that the genes also control the formation of specific proteins; eventually there emerged the idea of one gene being equivalent to one enzyme or protein. That is, for every protein molecule there is a separate gene. At this point we are confronted with two very fundamental questions: (1) How does the gene control the synthesis of a specific protein molecule such as an enzyme? (2) How does the gene duplicate itself?

The first approach of the biochemist was to learn of what material genes are composed. It was easy to determine the nature of all the chemical constituents in the cell; furthermore, determination of the composition of the genes followed easily since it was known that these occurred only in the nuclei of cells. It was necessary only to isolate the nuclei, then analyze them chemically. However, this information was not of great value. Although the inventory produced a list of chemical compounds, a role could not be assigned to them. The question as to which chemicals were genes and which were not was left unanswered.

An answer came from some quite unrelated studies by Griffith on types of pneumococci (bacteria causing pneumonia). Griffith worked with two types of pneumococci: one a smooth type, the other rough. The smooth type was virulent (that is, it caused pneumonia), whereas the rough form was nonvirulent and did not produce the disease. It was known that under certain conditions the nonvirulent stage became virulent. The question naturally arose as to how this occurred. Griffith killed the virulent strain and injected a rat with some of the dead cells, along with live nonvirulent strains, as shown in Fig. 2-9.

The nonvirulent strain was transformed into the virulent strain. This was accomplished in spite of the fact that the heated material was dead and therefore could not reproduce itself; if the heated material was injected alone, no pneumonia resulted. This could only mean that something in the heated material could convert the rough to the smooth form. Further experimentation showed that rats were not required for this transfer; it could be accomplished outside the living animal. Soon afterward the active chemical was isolated and found to be deoxyribonucleic acid (DNA) described in Chapter 1. This same material had been isolated from the nuclei of animal cells, but its role had not been recognized. Griffith's work pointed out a role for DNA: the ability to transform non-virulent bacteria into virulent bacteria. Once the nonvirulent

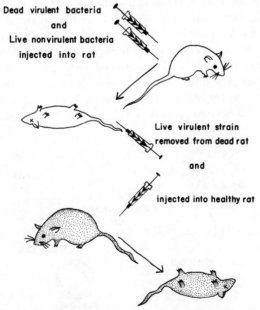

Dead virulent bacteria
and
Live nonvirulent bacteria
injected into rat

Live virulent strain
removed from dead rat

and

injected into healthy rat

Fig. 2-9. Demonstration of the participation of DNA in heredity.

strain was transformed, it then reproduced only virulent strains. This was an inherent trait. It has since been concluded (indeed, it might be deduced from the experiment just described with pneumonococci) that the role of DNA is to act as the master molecule that imparts particular characteristics to its successors—rather like a waffle iron.

This type of experiment has now been expanded to such an extent that we know DNA is the "long tape of segments of which the blueprint for the shaping of each protein is encoded." By such a definition we imply not only that the nucleus of a cell reproduces its own kind, but also that the development of an animal begins with a cell that has the potential to develop into *all* cell types (Fig. 2-10). What appears to happen is that part of this potential to synthesize all the enzymes of a cell is blocked and only certain ones are synthesized. For example, a cell may have the potential to make either muscle or cartilage. If the enzymes B making cartilage are suppressed, then muscle protein is made; alternately, if A is blocked, then bone (B) is produced.

Another possibility is that the cell also has the potential to become a cancer cell (C). In cancer we know that somehow a normal cell becomes a cancer cell. Now since we have said

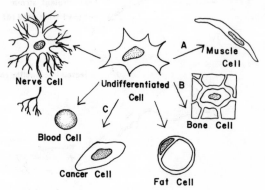

Fig. 2-10. Growth and differentiation processes.

that genes (or DNA) control the kinds of cells that are to be made, then the observation of an abnormal cell really means that the cause for its formation lies in the DNA molecule. The information that tells a cell how to form comes somehow from or through the master template: DNA. We do not know yet the details of the process, but progress is being made in our knowledge of how the DNA transfers its information resulting in the synthesis of proteins.

The first clue toward an understanding of the mechanism of protein synthesis came from studies of the incorporation of amino acids into proteins. When cells were added to amino acids that were labeled with carbon-14, radioactive protein was produced.

$$RC^{14}HCOOH + Cells \rightarrow C^{14}\text{-amino acids (in protein)}$$
$$\underset{NH_2}{|}$$

The problem was soon reduced to determining the steps leading from an amino acid to protein (X). It was known from other studies with organic acids that the following reaction occurred.

$$RCOOH + ATP \rightarrow RC\underset{\underset{O}{\|}}{-}AMP + PP$$

This has special significance here because the protein-synthesizing system required ATP, a special "energy-rich" compound (discussed in Chapter 3). Moreover, amino acids have a —COOH group similar to the compound listed in this example. As might have been expected, a similar reaction was shown in the activation of amino acids for protein synthesis. The enzyme responsible for this condensation occurs in the soluble portion of the cell (see Chapter 4 for discussion of various cell components). The resulting complex is an activated amino acid because extra energy is contained in the

$$\underset{\underset{NH_2}{|}}{\overset{\overset{H}{|}}{R\,C\,COOH}} + ATP \rightarrow \underset{\underset{NH_2}{|}}{\overset{\overset{H}{|}\overset{O}{\overset{\|}{}}}{R\,C\!-\!C\!-\!AMP}} + PP$$

Activated amino acid

$\overset{O}{\overset{\|}{}}$
$-C-AMP$ bond.   The ordinary peptide bond contains
about 3000 cal./mole, a relatively low figure.   Therefore, a
minimum of this amount of extra energy is needed to permit
protein synthesis to occur.   It might be assumed that by
adding several activated amino acids to a preparation from a
biological source, we would be able to synthesize a protein.
Unfortunately, this expedient failed, suggesting that an additional ingredient is needed.   Learning this, researchers then
attempted to isolate the required constituent; the key was
found to be a particular kind of RNA, called transfer RNA
(RNA transfer).   Thus, a reaction sequence may be written

$$aa + ATP \rightleftharpoons aa{-}AMP + PP + RNA\,transfer \rightarrow$$

Amino acid

$$aa{-}RNA\,transfer + AMP$$

The evidence indicates that there is a separate transfer RNA
for each of the twenty common amino acids.

The foregoing equation does not represent the final stage of
protein synthesis, since it only places the amino acid on the
transfer RNA.   The amino acid must be inserted into a protein
and in the correct position.   It was found that aa—RNA
transfer becomes associated with another RNA molecule, of a
very high molecular weight.   This RNA is composed of the
same compounds as the transfer RNA and is called the template RNA; because, like another waffle iron, it is the RNA
that determines the sequence of the amino acids.   The template may be represented as shown in Fig. 2-11.   The horizontal line represents the backbone of template RNA and
each of the letters a different base; A is adenine, U is uracil,

Fig. 2-11

G is quanine, and C is cytosine. It has been shown that it is possible to make a code for each of the twenty amino acids using only these four bases. If we assume that A in the template will only join with U or vice versa and G with C or vice versa (there is evidence that pairings are restricted in this fashion) then looking at site (1) in Fig. 2-11, as redrawn in Fig. 2-12a, we will find that this sequence will only combine with the sequence in Fig. 2-12b. If this combination is specific for a particular amino acid (there is some experimental evidence to support this assumption as outlined in Table 3-1), then another amino acid will join at each of the other sites. Next, the amino acids combine with the formation of a peptide bond, and when the protein is finally pieced together with the correct amino acid sequence, this is "zipped off" along with the transfer RNA's and the process can be started over again. Another way to look at this specificity is to assume the shapes given in Fig. 2-13a. If the template appears like Fig. 2-13b, then transfer RNA must be a complement in order to obtain a fit (Fig. 2-13c). This discussion completes one side of the coin, namely the placing of an amino acid onto an RNA molecule, transferring this to a template, and making the protein with a particular order of amino acids.

The other side of the coin concerns one of our earlier questions: how does the gene transmit its information to tell the

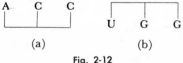

Fig. 2-12

template what kind of protein to synthesize? This appears to proceed as follows: DNA is known to give its code or message to another type of RNA, called messenger RNA. Messenger RNA then leaves the nucleus and carries the message received from DNA to template RNA, outside the cell nucleus. In some way the messenger RNA informs this (secondary) template what kind of protein is to be made. Apparently, the template RNA is not able to tell the amino acids how they should be arranged, i.e., what their sequence should be, until it gets a message from DNA by way of messenger RNA. Once it has received this message, it is able to cause the formation of a specific protein, meanwhile translating the four-unit language of the polynucleotides into the twenty-unit phraseology of the proteins, as illustrated in Table 2-1.

Nucleic acids therefore truly constitute the thread of life. They are the chemical constituents in the body that are the determinants of the continuity of life. The expression of this thread is made by the proteins. These are the visible features that we can ascribe to specificity. Thus, different cells in our bodies are unlike one another because of the protein makeup of that cell. Indeed, we are most fortunate that the process of

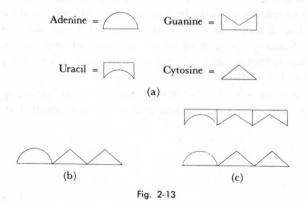

Fig. 2-13

evolution through natural selection accomplished such a marvelously distinct fabrication.

TABLE 2-1. Coding Equivalence between Nucleotides and Amino Acids in Protein Synthesis[a]

Amino acid	Code word	
	National Institutes of Health	New York University
Alanine	CCG	CUG CAG CCG
Arginine	CGC	GUC GAA GCC
Asparagine[b]	ACA	UAA CUA CAA
Aspartic acid[b]	ACA	GUA GCA
Cysteine[c]	UUG or UGG	GUU
Glutamic acid[d]	ACA AGA AUG	AAG AUG
Glutamine[d]	ACA	AGG ACA
Glycine	UGG	GUG GAG GCG
Histidine	ACC	AUC ACC
Isoleucine	UUA	UUA AAU
Leucine[e]	GUU CUU AUU (UUU)	UAU UUC UGU
Lysine	AAA AAC AAG AAU	AUA AAA
Methionine	UGA	UGA
Phenylalanine	UUU	UUU UUC
Proline	CCC CCU CCA CCG	CUC CCC CAC
Serine	UCG UUC UCC	CUU CCU ACG
Threonine	CAC CAA	UCA ACA CGC
Trytophan	UGG	UGG
Tryosine	UAU	AUU
Valine	UGU	UUG

[a] From Abelson, John, *Science* **139**, 775 (1963).

[b] The National Institutes of Health cannot as yet determine whether ACA represents aspartic acid or asparagine.

[c] It is not clear yet which of these possibilities is correct.

[d] The NIH group cannot as yet determine whether ACA represents glutamic acid or glutamine.

[e] Poly U will serve as a template for leucine in the absence of phenylalanine.

THE CELLULAR FURNACE

WE HAVE LISTED the principal materials out of which molecules in living structures are fabricated, and we have glimpsed the master dies (nucleic acids) and the operating machinery (enzyme systems) that are needed; many of these are enormously complex. In this chapter we will develop the chemical details of one of the most crucial of all activities that a cell or an organism pursues—that of getting energy to stay alive.

The abundance of life on this planet may cause us to overlook temporarily the fact, already mentioned, that all living organisms must ultimately derive their energy from sunlight. Most living organisms (except for green plants and a few photosynthetic microbes) receive their energy from some secondary source in the form of stored chemical energy. The nature of this stored energy, and of the processes for converting it into useful energy for maintaining life, will be our next major concern.

THE FUEL PROBLEM

Organisms vary widely in the details of their internal and external anatomy. No student of biology needs to reflect long on the distinctive gastrointenstinal features of an oyster, a chicken, or a cow to see this variety. Yet all of these creatures use essentially identical primary fuels. Whether mold or mosquito, mouse or man, the same molecules pass before the inquiring eye of the biochemist, and one is soon forced to conclude that despite the almost fantastic variety that exists in the morphology of organisms, and in individual molecules of proteins or nucleic acids that may serve as foods, there are only a handful of compounds that can furnish energy directly to a living cell.

Oxidation of Carbohydrates

The most important of the primary fuels is glucose. Most other foods, whatever their nature or source, are converted to glucose prior to further utilization by an organism or an individual cell. Because of the importance of glucose as a cellular fuel, we will consider first the chemical fate of this compound in metabolism.

A term used historically to describe the breakdown of glucose and other compounds is *catabolism*. The reverse process, that of building (synthesizing) larger molecules was called *anabolism*. Modern custom has been largely to ignore the question of breakdown or synthesis, and to lump both terms under the more general term *metabolism*, describing all of the chemical transformations that befall a given compound in an organism. Thus, this discussion might alternatively be titled *the oxidative metabolism of glucose*.

It should be noted at the outset that glucose is a true fuel; it is oxidized (burned) in the tissues. The final products of this reaction are CO_2 and H_2O.

$$C_6H_{12}O_6 + 6O_2 \rightarrow 6CO_2 + 6H_2O$$

A distinctive feature of biological oxidation, however, is that catalysts are needed, to permit the oxidation to proceed at body temperatures.

Glycolysis. The exact number of enzymes that act upon glucose molecules to transform them in tissues to carbon dioxide and water is probably not known; nearly a hundred different enzymes are presently recognized as cooperating in this process. The enzymes tend to operate in groups; members of these groups act in close unison. The first of these reaction patterns is called *glycolysis* ("dissolving of glucose"), so named because the alteration in the glucose molecule is nonoxidative in character. This is seen as glucose,

$$C_6H_{12}O_6 \rightarrow 2C_3H_6O_3$$

If ever an elephant labored to bring forth a mouse, this is an example; a full dozen steps are required here, each one being catalyzed by a different enzyme—all to effect a splitting of the glucose molecule. This is the complete story of glucose metabolism in lactic acid (milk-souring) bacteria.

In yeast the process is slightly more complicated: a close relative of lactic acid (pyruvic acid) is decarboxylated to acetaldehyde, then hydrogenated (reduced) to ethyl alcohol.

Pyruvic acid   Acetaldehyde   Ethyl alcohol (ethanol)

Oxidation of Pyruvic Acid: Krebs Tricarboxylic Acid Cycle. What happens to pyruvic acid reflects one of the major developments in the evolution of species. If we restrict our view for a moment to yeast and lactic acid bacteria, we see that carbohydrate metabolism grinds to a halt with the appearance of lactic or pyruvic acid or of ethanol. (The taste of sour milk or ethanol recalls the fact that the microorganisms producing these compounds eventually drown in their own waste products.) Only a little energy is produced in the breakdown of glucose to lactic acid or ethanol; most of the energy remains locked in the carbon skeletons of these products.

Higher animals, indeed most organisms, have developed differently, despite the fact that they also contain the glycolytic apparatus. In their tissues, additional enzymes are present that can oxidize pyruvic acid completely to CO_2 and H_2O, in a cyclic process that is best represented in the wordless sequence of Fig. 3-1. In this simplified diagram, compound A

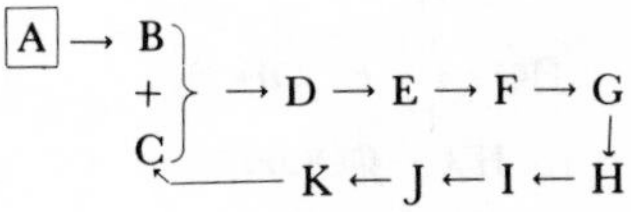

Fig. 3-1. Krebs tricarboxylic acid cycle (schematic diagram).

$$\boxed{A} \to B$$
$$+ \Big\} \to D \to E \to F \to G$$
$$C \qquad\qquad\qquad\qquad \downarrow$$
$$\longleftarrow K \leftarrow J \leftarrow I \leftarrow H$$

(pyruvic acid) breaks down to give a derivative of acetic acid (B), which condenses with another acid, oxaloacetic (C), to give citric acid (citrate) (D). Hence the name citric acid cycle, by which the Krebs cycle is sometimes called. The compounds that follow the breakdown of citrate are, in succession, *cis*-aconitate, isocitrate, oxalosuccinate, α-ketoglutarate, succinate, fumarate, and malate (K). Malate in its turn breaks down to regenerate oxaloacetate, which is compound C. Thus, the cycle can start over again, using a fresh molecule of compound A; the first molecule of A has meanwhile been consumed through this cyclic process. The fresh molecule of A (pyruvate), which comes from glucose via glycolysis, is converted to B, and then cycled to yield carbon·dioxide and water, with one of the intermediates (C) re-emerging at each turn of the cycle and accepting a fresh molecule of B until all the glucose is used. The cycle in its more conventional form is given in Fig. 3-2.

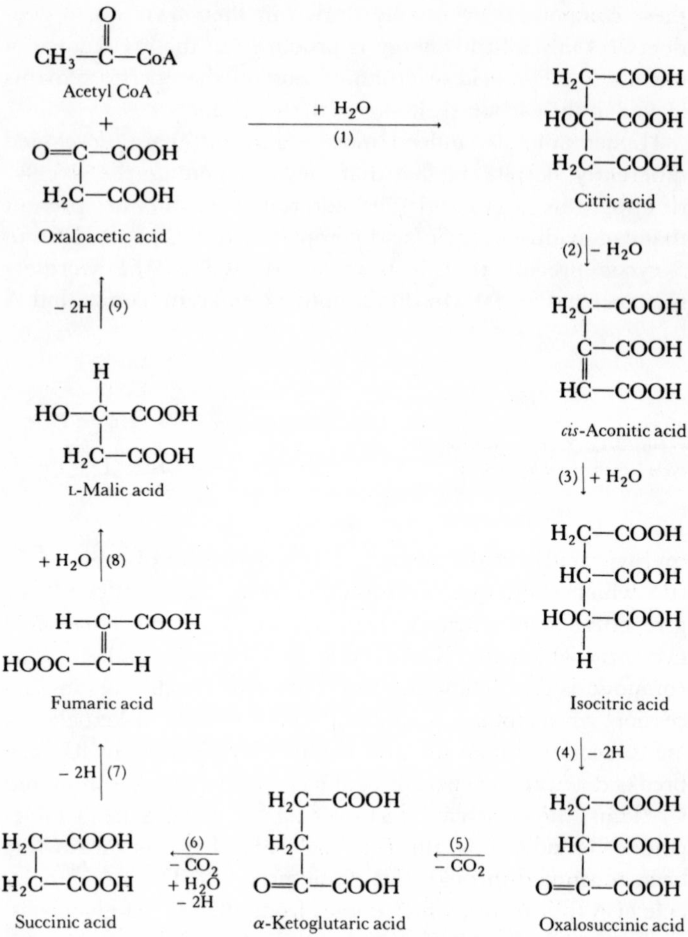

Fig. 3-2. Krebs tricarboxylic acid cycle (detailed).

The term "-ic acid" has been used, in conformation to organic chemical nomenclature. It is recognized, however, that these compounds probably exist as salts in tissues, where the pH of cell solutions is often far removed from the strongly acidic conditions that would be needed to maintain these compounds as true acids. Henceforth these and other tissue acids will be referred to as "-ates."

This cycle, discovered by Krebs and Johnson in England in 1937, soon became popularly known as the Krebs cycle. The elegance of the scheme caught the world-wide interest and imagination of biochemists soon after its discovery. Within a few years investigators in many countries had examined various animals and plants, and had discovered Krebs cycle activity to be present and apparently operative. Indeed, as new forms were tested, it appeared that, except for some microorganisms, there were very few organisms that did not contain the Krebs cycle. For his efforts in charting this important route of metabolism, Professor Krebs was honored by receiving the Nobel prize in medicine in 1953; he was also knighted by Queen Elizabeth.

Pentose Cycle. A less intensively used, but nonetheless significant route of glucose breakdown is the *pentose cycle*. Its role may be partly one of synthesis of appropriate carbon chains in the cell; but this pathway can also yield energy via the oxidative route, hence is discussed here.

Oxidation in the pentose cycle features an attack on glucose-6-phosphate, by yielding first an acid, 6-phosphogluconic acid; then a decarboxylation and another oxidation follow, to form a pentose phosphate.

The further metabolism of pentose phosphate involves a redistribution of the sugar chains of several molecules into C_7, C_6, C_4, and C_3 units, as outlined in Fig. 3-3. (Glucose-6-phosphate and other hexose phosphates participating are here abbreviated C_6P; 6 molecules are employed for ease in explanation.) Reaction 1 (Fig. 3-3) comprises the two oxi-

$$
\begin{array}{c}
\text{H} \\
| \\
\text{C}{=}\text{O} \\
| \\
\text{HCOH} \\
| \\
\text{HOCH} \\
| \\
\text{HCOH} \\
| \\
\text{HCOH} \\
| \\
\text{H}_2\text{COPO}_3\text{H}_2 \\
\text{Glucose-6-phosphate}
\end{array}
\xrightarrow[-2\text{H}]{+\text{H}_2\text{O}}
\begin{array}{c}
\text{O} \\
\| \\
\text{COH} \\
| \\
\text{HCOH} \\
| \\
\text{HOCH} \\
| \\
\text{HCOH} \\
| \\
\text{HCOH} \\
| \\
\text{COPO}_3\text{H}_2 \\
\text{6-Phosphogluconic} \\
\text{acid}
\end{array}
\xrightarrow{-2\text{H}}
\begin{array}{c}
\text{HC}{=}\text{O} \\
| \\
\text{HCOH} \quad +\ \text{CO}_2 \\
| \\
\text{HCOH} \\
| \\
\text{HCOH} \\
| \\
\text{COPO}_3\text{H}_2 \\
\text{Ribose-5-phosphate} \\
\text{(a pentose)}
\end{array}
$$

dative (dehydrogenation) steps mentioned above. Two molecules of C_5P then rearrange to produce C_7P and C_3P. The C_7 and C_3 units rearrange further to form a tetrose phosphate, C_4P, *plus a molecule of* C_6P. This C_6P is in equilibrium with one of the C_6P's used at the start; we see that a molecule of starting material has been regenerated. Meanwhile, the C_4P that was also produced at this step is able to combine with a third molecule of C_5P (formed in Reaction 3, Fig. 3-3). This $C_4P + C_5P$ union produces C_3P plus a *second* unit of the starting material, C_6P.

The overall result of the metabolic activities in the left half of the diagram has thus been to employ three molecules of C_6P in a series of reactions that, in effect, regenerate two and one-half of the molecules; a C_3P unit is left over, shown at the extreme left of Fig. 3-3. By the doubling of the entire plan and insertion of reactions 4, 5, and 6, the two C_3P units that would remain are joined, as shown, to form a hexose diphosphate, C_6P_2, which loses a phosphate group readily to form a *fifth* molecule of C_6P. Hence, the sum

$$6C_6P \longrightarrow 6C_5P \longrightarrow 5C_6P$$
$$\searrow 6C_1$$

This reaction is also a cycle, since some of the starting material is regenerated at each turn, with C_1 (CO_2) being formed as an additional product. This cycle (the pentose cycle) can operate independently of glycolysis and the Krebs cycle, although the pentose cycle and the Krebs cycle are also able to function in interrelated fashion; when triose phosphate (C_3P)

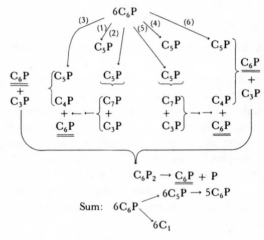

Fig. 3-3. Pentose cycle.

is produced, it may rearrange as outlined in Fig. 3-4 for pentose cycle metabolism or it may be oxidized to pyruvic acid, then to CO_2 and H_2O via the Krebs cycle.

Entner-Doudoroff Pathway. This route, named for its discoverers, is yet a third pathway of glucose oxidation, slightly different from glycolysis. It is illustrated in Fig. 3-4. The splitting of the hexose chain occurs through an attack on the compound 2-keto-3-deoxy-6-phosphogluconic acid (which is formed from glucose). The C_3 products, pyruvate and gly-

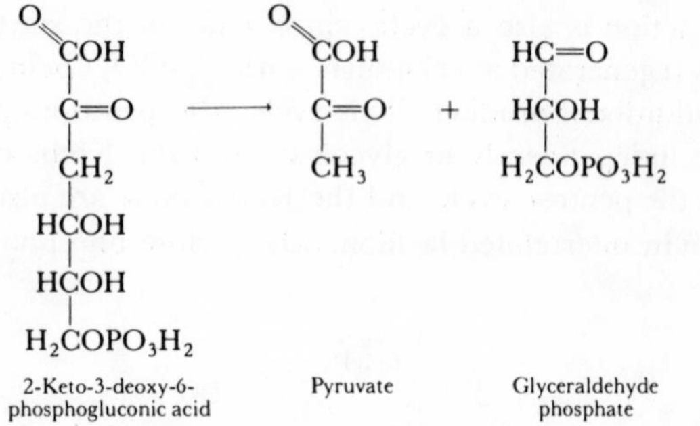

$$\underset{\substack{\text{2-Keto-3-deoxy-6-} \\ \text{phosphogluconic acid}}}{\begin{array}{c} O \\ \backslash \\ COH \\ | \\ C{=}O \\ | \\ CH_2 \\ | \\ HCOH \\ | \\ HCOH \\ | \\ H_2COPO_3H_2 \end{array}} \longrightarrow \underset{\text{Pyruvate}}{\begin{array}{c} O \\ \backslash \\ COH \\ | \\ C{=}O \\ | \\ CH_3 \end{array}} + \underset{\substack{\text{Glyceraldehyde} \\ \text{phosphate}}}{\begin{array}{c} HC{=}O \\ | \\ HCOH \\ | \\ H_2COPO_3H_2 \end{array}}$$

Fig. 3-4. Entner-Doudoroff scheme of carbohydrate metabolism.

ceraldehyde phosphate, may be fed either into the pentose cycle or into the Krebs cycle.

The Entner-Doudoroff pathway may be considered as a variant form of glycolysis. This route is without great significance in most organisms, although a few microorganisms appear to employ it for carbohydrate oxidation. In most other forms, glycolysis followed by the Krebs cycle carries the bulk of the glucose metabolic "traffic"; the pentose cycle generally accounts for about one-tenth to one-fourth of the total glucose oxidized.

Oxidation of Fats

Fats constitute the second great class of foodstuffs. Through an exacting series of investigations by many scientists beginning with Knoop in 1904 and culminating in the efforts of Green and co-workers in 1953, it has been established that the long-chain fatty acids that occur in natural fats are oxidized in body cells in a "scissoring" fashion such as that depicted in Fig. 3-5. The molecular units are decreased by two carbon atoms at a time. Thus, the eight-carbon fatty acid, octanoic acid, is shorn of two carbon atoms *which comprise the same compound as compound B in the Krebs cycle* (see Fig.

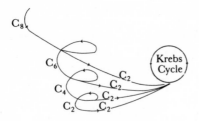

Fig. 3-5. Fatty acid helix.

3-1). Compound B, a derivative of acetic acid, goes directly into the Krebs cycle, where it is oxidized to carbon dioxide and water just as if it had arisen from carbohydrate. The remaining fatty acid residue, which is the six-carbon caproic acid, undergoes the same "scissoring" treatment, producing another unit of acetic acid, and so on to the end. Because each remaining fatty acid unit is smaller than the preceding one, this diagram is referred to as the fatty acid helix rather than a true cycle, even though the process is generally cyclic in character.

Oxidation of Proteins

When proteins are digested to their constituent amino acids, the amino acids are also broken down via the Krebs cycle. Various amino acid-oxidizing enzymes are present that form products that are components of the Krebs cycle (compounds A, H, and I, J, K, or C of Fig. 3-1). Thus, alanine, valine, and serine are oxidized via the "C_3" or three-carbon gateway (Fig. 3-6); glutamic acid and several other amino acids gain entry through α-ketoglutarate, the "C_5" compound in the Krebs cycle; whereas threonine and aspartic acid disappear through one of the "C_4" thresholds related to oxaloacetic acid. The great bulk of the twenty or more amino acid building blocks of proteins can thus be utilized, when eaten in

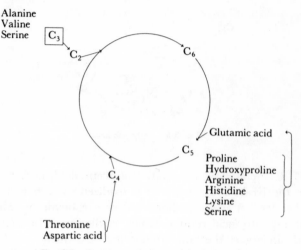

Fig. 3-6.   Protein metabolism and the Krebs cycle.

excess (as in a steak, etc.), for energy in the living organism. Thus proteins, which constitute the third great class of foodstuffs, also contribute to the energy pool by the same major metabolic route as do the other two food classes.

THE FLAME

We have seen how glucose is the fuel of choice for most living organisms. Let us now consider the means whereby this cellular fuel is oxidized. It was discovered several decades ago that if glucose is burned in a calorimeter, the total amount of heat produced is exactly the same as that produced when glucose is oxidized in living tissues; the same amounts of water and carbon dioxide are also formed. The equation,

$$C_6H_{12}O_6 + 6O_2 \rightarrow 6CO_2 + 6H_2O$$

describes cellular oxidation of glucose; indeed, if the notation

$$+ 690,000 \text{ cal./mole}$$

is added, the situation is described exactly.

If a person were to eat only glucose, the calorie yield per gram would be $690,000/180 = 3800$ cal. $= 3.8$ kcal. A person requiring 2500 kcal./day could therefore obtain it from eating 658 g. (about 1.5 lb.) of glucose per day.

The biological oxidation of glucose differs greatly in detail, however, from the more straightforward burning of this compound in a calorimeter. Whereas burning in a calorimeter is a simple reaction that proceeds at high temperatures, body oxidation of glucose and other fuels proceeds at body temperatures, and in many steps. Moreover, for each step there is a separate enzyme that catalyzes each reaction.

There is another important difference: biological oxidation yields its useful energy through the burning of hydrogen to form water. Although the carbon of the organic compound in question gradually increases its oxidation state during the process, finally reaching the oxidation level of $+4$ at carbon dioxide; the significant energy-yielding steps inevitably feature oxidation of hydrogen. This is "stretched out" in great detail. Although individual enzymes may react somewhat differently, the general biological oxidation patterns proceed as shown in in Table 3-1.

The total calorie yield lies very close to the figure obtained by burning hydrogen in an open flame: 57,800 cal./mole of water vapor formed. To calculate the total energy available from oxidizing a mole of glucose, we must regard Table 3-1 as only one-twelfth complete: we need to react a new primary dehydrogenase with the 6-phosphogluconate produced from step 1 of the pentose cycle (see page 58); this produces pentose phosphate (plus hydrogen), which can now traverse steps 2–5 outlined in Table 3-1. The pentose phosphate is normally redistributed through the pentose cycle (Fig. 3-3), the regenerated hexose oxidized, and so on until all six carbon atoms of the original glucose molecule are oxidized to CO_2 and H_2O. Thus, the total energy yield from a mole of glucose is 57,330 × 12 = 688,000 cal., in 5 × 12 = 60 individual oxidation steps as listed in Table 3-1.

TABLE 3-1.   General Outline of Biological Oxidation

1. Hydrogen is removed from the subject molecule (called the substrate). If glucose-6-phosphate is the substrate, glucose-6-PO_4 $\rightarrow$ 6-phosphogluconate +	2H
This reaction requires an enzyme which is called a primary	*dehydrogenase* (calorie yield = 5080/mole)
2. The dehydrogenase, with 2H bound to the enzyme protein, transfers its hydrogen to another enzyme, which is called another	*dehydrogenase*[a] (calorie yield = 12,500/mole)
3. A third enzyme, containing iron in the form known as cytochrome, accepts the hydrogen from the second dehydrogenase. This new enzyme is called a	*mediator* (calorie yield = 14,350/mole)
4. The mediator now transfers the hydrogen to other iron-containing enzymes, called	*oxidases* (calorie yield = 13,400/mole)
5. Oxygen is combined with hydrogen at the surface of the enzymes to form	H_2O (calorie yield = 12,000/mole)
Total calorie yield	57,330/mole

[a]These dehydrogenases that accept hydrogen from the primary dehydrogenases frequently contain the vitamin riboflavin and are often called *flavoproteins*.

Thus, a prominent feature of biological oxidation is the separation of the overall reaction into small steps. If one could utilize these parcels individually, there might seem to be some "purpose" to this excessive fragmentation process, though as scientists we should be cautious about imputing teleologic ends to scientific events, lest we occasionally be misled by hastily concocted notions, which may seem plausible yet are not able to withstand rigorous checking. Sometimes reaction mechanisms in biology seem foolish to the synthetic chemist, who may have learned to effect a given organic synthesis by quite a different route than the ones employed in nature. Having urged this caution upon ourselves, we will now go on to say that the small bursts of energy referred to in Fig. 3-1 are indeed conserved in small, discrete packets. These packets are characterized and defined in the language of chemistry in the following paragraph.

In nonliving, nonenzymic oxidations, carbon-hydrogen bonds are broken and yield their energy directly. There is a different process in the cell whereby this energy is converted, conserved, and then used later by forming an intermediate "energy-storage" compound. Such a compound contains a different type of chemical bond; biochemists often refer to these "packages" as *energy-rich* bonds that usually include phosphate groups. These energy-rich bonds occur in a dozen or more compounds, which are nearly all interconvertible. The most common of these is adenosine triphosphate, abbre-

Adenosine triphosphate (ATP)

TABLE 3-2. Energy-Rich Compounds of Biological Importance

Adenosine triphosphate	(ATP)	
Adenosine diphosphate	(ADP)	1,3-Diphosphoglyceric acid (1,3-PGA)
Guanosine triphosphate	(GTP)	Phosphoenolpyruvic acid (PEP)
Guanosine diphosphate	(GDP)	Acetyl phosphate
Uridine triphosphate	(UTP)	Creatine phosphate
Uridine diphosphate	(UDP)	Arginine phosphate
Cytidine triphosphate	(CTP)	Imidazole phosphate

viated ATP. ATP acts as a "reservoir" of energy-rich compounds. These are listed in Table 3-2.

An additional energy-rich compound is acetyl coezyme A. (Coenzyme A and several of its derivatives were discovered by Professor F. Lipmann. For this work, together with his development of the concept of energy-rich bonds, he shared the Nobel Prize with Krebs in 1953.) Acetyl coenzyme A, abbreviated AcCoA, differs from those listed in Table 3-2 in that it does not contain phosphorus. It is best identified as compound B of Fig. 3-1, in the Krebs cycle.

All of these energy-rich compounds are characterized by extreme instability in water, hydrolyzing to give up 8000 to 15,000 cal./mole to the surroundings. Nearly all of them are anhydrides with the structure of a phosphate anhydride.

When the surroundings are "right," that is, when they contain reactants in the proper mixture and when the appropriate enzymes are present, these calories can be used to synthesize cellular constituents or to effect muscular work, nerve transmission, or any other processes in the body that require expenditure of energy. These activities are dramatized in Fig.

Phosphate anhydride (ATP, etc.)

Organic acid anhydride

3-7. When ATP provides the required energy, the terminal phosphate bond breaks, and the attendant energy is released as if we had released the energy stored in a coiled spring (Fig. 3-8). Reaction 1 in Fig. 3-8 is the one releasing the energy for cellular work; reaction 2 is the reverse, that is, the spring is being "coiled," by coupling a phosphorylation of ADP to inorganic phosphate. The energy for the synthesis of ATP comes from the oxidation of glucose, or more correctly, from

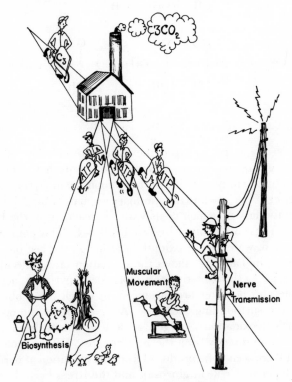

Fig. 3-7. The power plant—Krebs cycle.

the oxidation of hydrogen via the steps outlined in Table 3-1. The formation of ATP is not a continuous process; so far as the scheme in Table 3-1 is concerned, ATP is formed only at steps 1, 2, and 3 or 4, for a total yield of 3 molecules of ATP for each 2H oxidized.

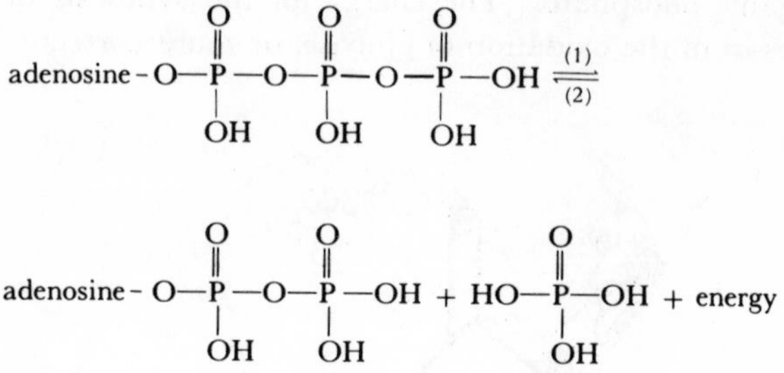

$$\text{adenosine} - \text{O}-\overset{\overset{\displaystyle O}{\|}}{\underset{\underset{\displaystyle OH}{|}}{P}}-\text{O}-\overset{\overset{\displaystyle O}{\|}}{\underset{\underset{\displaystyle OH}{|}}{P}}-\text{O}-\overset{\overset{\displaystyle O}{\|}}{\underset{\underset{\displaystyle OH}{|}}{P}}-\text{OH} \underset{(2)}{\overset{(1)}{\rightleftharpoons}}$$

$$\text{adenosine} - \text{O}-\overset{\overset{\displaystyle O}{\|}}{\underset{\underset{\displaystyle OH}{|}}{P}}-\text{O}-\overset{\overset{\displaystyle O}{\|}}{\underset{\underset{\displaystyle OH}{|}}{P}}-\text{OH} + \text{HO}-\overset{\overset{\displaystyle O}{\|}}{\underset{\underset{\displaystyle OH}{|}}{P}}-\text{OH} + \text{energy}$$

Fig. 3-8

It is of interest to trace the overall production of ATP during glucose oxidation. Reviewing the steps that involve the consumption or production of this compound in glycolysis and the Krebs cycle, we find the summary given in Table 3-3. Turn again to Fig. 3-2, which deals with the reactions of the Krebs cycle. These are summarized in Table 3-4. This emphasizes the role of water in the oxidation; although the last balanced equation in Table 3-4 shows the formation of 2 molecules of water during the oxidation of a molecule of pyruvate, actually 5 molecules of water are produced, of which 3 are obtained from the surrounding medium. As is characteristic of most biological oxidations, oxygen is derived chiefly from water rather than directly from the atmosphere. Fifteen molecules of ATP are seen to be produced from the oxidation of pyruvate (= 30 per molecule of glucose), and the Krebs cycle is again observed to contribute a much greater proportion of the total energy from glucose than does glycolysis. If we assign 8000 cal. to each molecule of ATP formed, then $38 \times 8000 =$ ap-

TABLE 3.3. ATP Formation During Glycolysis Followed by Krebs Cycle Operation

	Yield of ATP moles
Glycolysis	
(a) Two moles of ATP are required for the initial phosphorylation of glucose $\rightarrow$ glucose-6-PO_4 $\rightarrow$ fructose-1, 6-diphosphate	-2
(b) Four moles of ATP are formed during the splitting of glucose-6-PO_4 $\rightarrow$ 2 lactic acid $\qquad 2 \times 2 =$ (these phosphorylations are not dependent on net H oxidation)	$+4$
(c) Six moles of ATP are formed during oxidation of H in the conversion of 2 lactic acid $\rightarrow$ 2 pyruvic acid $\qquad 3 \times 2 =$	$+6$
Further Oxidations in the Krebs Cycle (see also Fig. 3-2)	
(d) Six moles of ATP are formed during oxidation of H in the conversion of 2 pyruvic acid $\rightarrow$ 2 acetyl CoA $\qquad 3 \times 2 =$	$+6$
(e) Six moles of ATP are formed during oxidation of H in the conversion of isocitric to α-ketoglutaric acid $\qquad 3 \times 2 =$	$+6$
(f) Eight moles of ATP are formed during oxidation of H in the conversion of α-ketoglutaric to succinic acid $\quad 4 \times 2 =$ (there is an extra step here, so that the usual 3 phosphorylations are exceeded)	$+8$
(g) Four moles of ATP are formed during oxidation of H in the conversion of succinic to fumaric acid $\qquad 2 \times 2 =$	$+4$
(h) Six moles of ATP are formed during oxidation of H in the conversion of malic to oxaloacetic acid $\qquad 3 \times 2 =$	$+6$
Total	38

prox. 304,000 cal. conserved for useful work during the generation of 688,000 cal. in glucose oxidation. This represents a conversion efficiency of 44%—a high figure when compared to energy conversion in other types of machines.

Similar calculations may be made for energy conversion by the pentose cycle; here 3 ATP is produced concurrently with the oxidation of each pair of hydrogen atoms. Since twelve pairs of hydrogen atoms are oxidized per molecule of glucose, 36 molecules of ATP are produced, for a conversion efficiency of 42%.

When the fatty acid, palmitate, is burned, 131 moles of ATP are formed during the oxidation of one mole of the acid,

TABLE 3-4. Summary of Krebs Cycle Reactions as Described in Fig. 3-2.

Reaction no.[a]	ATP produced, molecules	H_2O consumed, molecules	H released, atoms	CO_2 released, molecules
"0"[b]	3	0	2	1
1	0	1	0	0
2	0	−1 (released)	0	0
3	0	1	0	0
4 5	3	0	2	1
6	4	1	2	1
7	2	0	2	0
8	0	1	0	0
9	3	0	2	0
Total	15	3	10	3

In summary,
$$CH_3COCOOH + 3H_2O \rightarrow 10H + 3CO_2 (+ 5H_2O)$$
      Pyruvic acid
by rearranging,
$$C_3H_4O_3 + 5O^c \rightarrow 2H_2O + CO_2$$

[a] Refers to reactions in Fig. 3-2.
[b] Pyruvate → AcCoA.
[c] Five oxygen atoms are equivalent to 10 H.

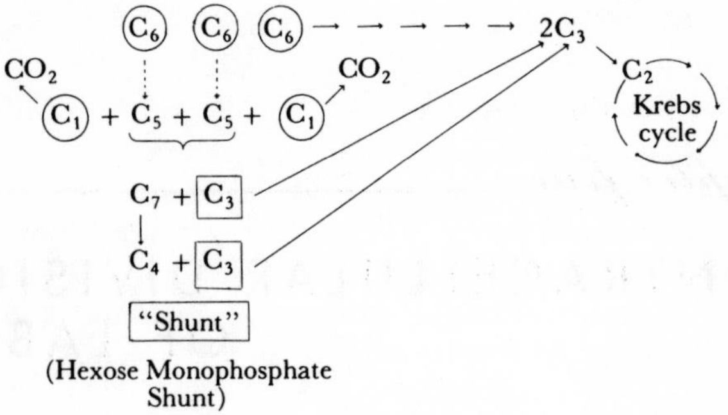

Fig. 3-9. Summary of carbohydrate metabolism schemes, including Krebs cycle.

having a calorific value of 2,400,000 cal., for a conversion efficiency of 42%. Similar calculations of energy yield from amino acid oxidations are difficult because of the varying sizes of individual molecules; nevertheless, they are in the same general range.

It is to be realized that the several pathways of carbohydrate metabolism usually occur in a living organism. The relations between the pentose cycle, Krebs cycle, and glycolysis are shown in Fig. 3-9.

chapter four

INTRACELLULAR DIVISION
OF LABOR

WE HAVE STRESSED that living cells contain a large number of enzymes. There is at this date, little knowledge of the exact number that may be present; a figure of at least 10,000 *different* enzymes seems not unreasonable, since about 1000 have already been discovered and partially purified.

Careful calculation has shown that there is a real housing problem if we attempt to find room for all the biocatalysts that may simultaneously exist in the cell. This problem may be eased somewhat by recent findings that enzymes exist in hierarchies or complexes; there is a close physical association within the cell of many of the enzymes that are otherwise considered as a group because of their related chemical activities, for example, Krebs cycle enzymes.

Cellular Inclusions: Organelles

It is worthwhile to digress briefly at this point to discuss some of the various morphological units that appear within the cell. Although these have long been familiar to classical biologists, in recent years, this field of research has also yielded information of value to chemists, and has produced a fusion of interest among persons working in the two fields.

If one examines a cellular preparation on a microscopic slide under low to medium magnification, he is impressed at once by certain structural entities that are clearly visible. As is shown in the generalized drawing of a cell in Fig. 4-1 the largest object is the moonlike *nucleus*, familiar to anyone who has looked at nearly any tissue preparation under a magnifying lens. Since the nuclei are relatively dense, they can be centrifuged away from other cell material in gravitational fields of a few hundred times gravity.

All cellular material outside the nucleus is called cell sap, or *cytoplasm*. The cytoplasm was at one time considered to be relatively formless; however, with modern advances in microscopy and centrifugation techniques, it has been possible to separate and identify several other bodies from the rest of the cytoplasm. When this is done according to the scheme shown in Fig. 4-2, the first fraction of the cytoplasm to precipitate contains the *mitochondria*, or "large granules" (after removal of the nuclei). The mitochondria, which are seen in Fig. 4-3,

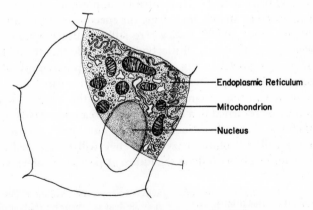

Fig. 4-1.   Cross-section of a generalized cell.

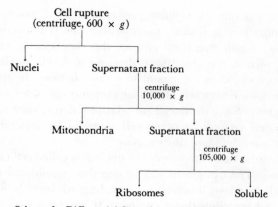

Scheme for Differential Centrifugation of Cell Constituents

Fig. 4-2. Scheme for differential centrifugation of cell constituents.

are small compared to the nucleus, but larger than many other small cellular inclusions. The mitochondria precipitate readily in a centrifuge at $10,000 \times g$[1]; the supernatant fraction may be returned to the centrifuge and additional material precipitated by merely increasing the speed up to gravitational fields of about $50,000 \times g$, where still smaller particles, the *ribosomes* (microsomes; "little bodies") predominate. These may be recognized in Fig. 4-3, which is a photograph of an electron microscope section of a cell; thus, the ribosomes are visible at extreme magnification. Again, the "soup" or cell sap may be returned to a centrifuge and treated in fields up to $150,000 \times g$; another fraction settles out here. These are usually called "soluble enzymes"; they will undoubtedly be characterized more fully in the future as pertinent information

---

[1] g = a force equal to the pull of gravity. An appreciation of the magnitude of the gravitational fields used here may be had by realizing that airplane stunt pilots frequently lose consciousness at 8 to $10 \times g$.

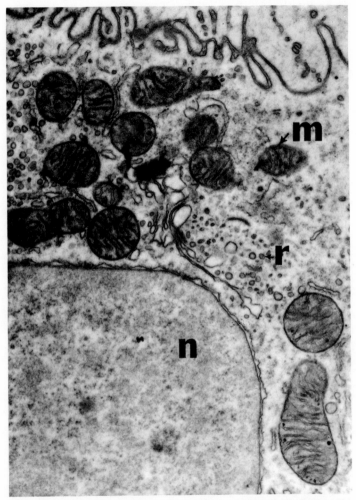

Fig. 4-3. Electron photomicrograph of cell fractions.

Electron micrograph of a limited field viewing chief cells from the stomach lining of a frog. A portion of the nucleus is visible at *n*, mitochondria at *m*, and ribosomes at *r*. Magnification = 50,000.

is accumulated. Progress has been slower with the characterization of the tinier units, since they are so small they cannot be seen individually even with the aid of the high magnification (50,000-fold and over) that is possible with an electron microscope.

The significance of these treatments lies in the fact that cytochemists (cell chemists) have discovered that this type of separation will almost completely separate the cell fractions not only morphologically, but also on the basis of differing chemical activities; the enzymes necessary for expediting several types of chemical operations are of different size, and *reside at different places within the cell.* Thus, if we summarize

TABLE 4-1. Inventory of Cell Fractions According to Morphology, Centrifugability, and Type of Chemical Activity Catalyzed

Cell fraction	Approx. diameter of particles μ	Centrifuged by gravitational field, $\times g$	Type of chemical activity displayed
Whole cell (mammalian)	20		
Nuclei	5–7	600	Contain all of the cellular genetic apparatus, including DNA and associated protein
Mitochondria[a]	0.5	10,000	Contain Krebs cycle enzymes, virtually all oxidative phosphorylation catalysts and related oxidizing enzymes; all enzymes associated with electron (hydrogen) transport
Ribosomes	0.1	50,000	Enzymes promoting protein synthesis; contain RNA
"Soluble" enzymes	< 0.1	105,000	All pentose cycle activity; glycolysis enzymes

[a] Length, 3–4 μ.

these separations, the kind of information shown in Table 4-1 is obtained.

When separation is virtually complete, it is evident that Nature has designed the respective cellular inclusions, or organelles, to carry out specific tasks for the cell's economy, in a division-of-labor plan that is noteworthy indeed. The presence of "our ancestors" (the genetic code) as DNA in the nucleus is so exclusive as to leave no room for doubt in the minds of experimenters as to its singular presence in cell nuclei; also in the nuclei is the complete apparatus for transmitting hereditary characteristics, including the mechanism governing cell division.

Enzymes of the Krebs cycle, which has been referred to as the intracellular furnace or power plant, are seen to be housed exclusively in the mitochondria. It is of great interest, and is probably of great significance as well, that the oxidative phosphorylation apparatus and the electron transport mechanisms are housed cheek-by-jowl with the Krebs cycle enzymes in the mitochondria. Not to be exceeded in this mutually exclusive classification scheme is the synthesis of protein in the ribosomes—other fractions of the cells are completely lacking in this ability, but the ribosomal fraction can build protein even when separated from the rest of the cell.

Data allocating pentose cycle enzymes and glycolysis enzymes exclusively to the "soluble" fractions of the cell are not so compelling in apparent reasons for their particular places of residence, yet there can be no doubt of the validity of the observations; enzymes that are able to promote glycolysis or the pentose cycle are simply not to be found, even in traces, in mitochondria or nuclei, whereas activity of these enzymes is complete within the "soluble" fraction even in the absence of other cell fractions.

Some leaders in this field have suggested, as individual organelles have been fragmented further and analyzed both for biological and chemical function, that there are "elemental particles" (not to be confused with chemical elements) within the cell that mirror entire phases of activity of the intact cell. The work of such persons is surely pointed in the direction of reconstructing the whole from chemically identifiable, individual parts. The focus of interest for the cell biologist and the biochemist has sharpened much, having grown very small in individual size but very broad in scope. A barrier for both groups of scientists in the past has been the necessary *organization* of a large number of molecules into units that have a definite physiological function—a major requirement for the condition of life.

EXTENDING THE THREAD

AN UNUSUAL CHARACTERISTIC, almost unique to living organisms, is the extreme dependence of one chemical event upon another in extensive sequences. The intimate relations in our thread of life between nucleic acids and proteins have already illustrated this quality of nature. The efficiency of the cellular furnace is a further example of a close link between structure and function. The juxtaposition of one enzyme to another permits these reactions to occur. Such reactions lead to the synthesis of other cellular materials such as carbohydrates and lipids. Proteins are intimately associated with this extension of the thread since they are the catalysts guiding the synthesis of other important constituents.

We can classify the general reactions occurring in living organisms into two groups—catabolism and anabolism. Catabolism has been defined (page 53) as the degradation of chemical compounds to smaller molecules, generally producing energy; catabolic reactions predominate in the cellular furnace. Anabolism is the synthesis of larger molecules from smaller ones; this process is the extension of the thread. A competition exists for molecules to determine the path by which they may be used—synthesis or breakdown. One of the remarkable facets of this competition is the rigid control that exists. Under various conditions, the biological system "knows" exactly how much effort needs to be expended in each route.

Photosynthesis

During the course of evolution, one of the important requirements was to devise a way whereby one of the principal chemical constituents, carbohydrates, could be synthesized. Fortunately such a mechanism developed. This process, known as photosynthesis, has been developed by green plants to carry out the conversion of light energy from the sun into chemical energy, in a most remarkable way. We have already noted this reaction, which in its simplest form is written as the reverse of glucose oxidation.

$$6CO_2 + 6H_2O \xrightarrow[\text{chlorophyll}]{\text{light}} C_6H_{12}O_6 + 6O_2$$

(Each year photosynthesis uses 396,000,000,000 tons of carbon dioxide on this planet to make 270,000,000,000 tons of glucose.) In photosynthesis two distinct but related processes occur. One is the conversion of carbon dioxide to carbohydrate. The other is the conversion of light energy into chemical energy. Possibly another way to describe this is as a series of synthetic reactions driven by light.

Several years ago, the Nobel Laureate Melvin Calvin, together with his group at the University of California, devised a scheme to learn what compounds carbon dioxide is converted into prior to becoming carbohydrate. We may visualize the scheme somewhat as follows:

$$C^{14}O_2 + X \xrightarrow[\text{chlorophyll}]{\text{light}} XC^{14}O_2 \rightarrow \rightarrow \rightarrow \text{carbohydrate}$$

where X is a compound that combines with carbon dioxide. Experimentally, if we place a green plant in the light in the presence of radioactive carbon dioxide, we should be able, assuming that the plant reacts with ("fixes") CO_2, to isolate the compounds formed. If we stop the reaction or remove a sample after a sufficiently short time, only XCO_2 would become radioactive, due to combination of radioactive CO_2 with the plant-synthesized compound X. Essentially the experiment consists of placing algae in a solution containing $C^{14}O_2$, then (substituting a light bulb for the sun) illuminating the mixture. (Fig. 5-1 depicts this process.) By devising a scheme

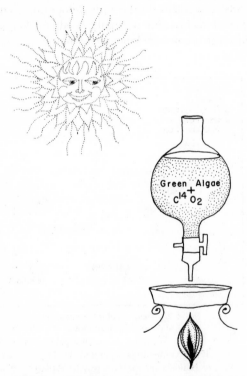

Fig. 5-1. Diagram of experimental procedure for effecting photosynthesis.

whereby at a particular time samples can be removed and chemical reactions immediately halted, we may then isolate the radioactive compounds at our leisure. Boiling alcohol serves to kill the plant tissues when this is desired. Since the compounds of interest are present in the plant in minute amounts, they are separated on paper chromatograms. Next we employ a method to learn where the C^{14}-containing compounds occur on the chromatogram. This process is called radioautography (see Fig. 5-2). Although several individual compounds are evident on the radioautogram, even after the short time of incubation normally used, further shortening of the interval results in labeling of fewer and fewer com-

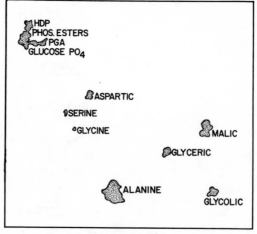

Fig. 5-2. Diagram of radioautograph
of a paper chromatogram.

An X-ray film is placed on top of a paper chromatogram. If the compounds separated on the chromatogram are radioactive, the film will be exposed. This has occurred wherever a dark spot appears in the above picture.

pounds; as the exposure to $C^{14}O_2$ is progressively diminished, a situation is eventually reached where only one compound (presumably the first one to be formed: $XC^{14}O_2$) contains radioactivity.

Calvin's group found that the first stable compound they

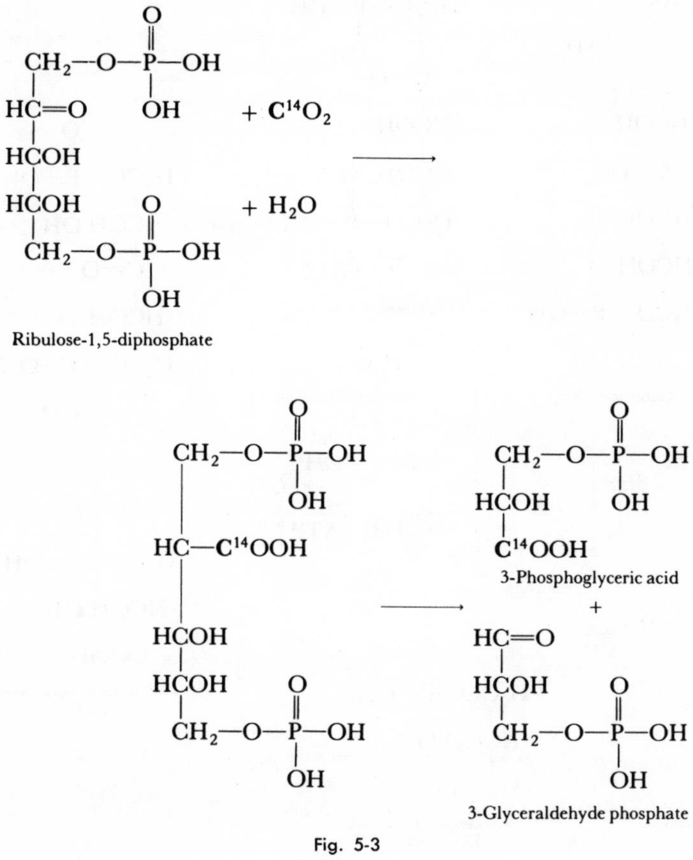

Ribulose-1,5-diphosphate

3-Phosphoglyceric acid

3-Glyceraldehyde phosphate

Fig. 5-3

could isolate was 3-phosphoglyceric acid, and that all of the isotope was initially in the carboxyl group. Present evidence suggests that X is a five-carbon sugar, ribulose diphosphate. The reactions are shown in Fig. 5-3.

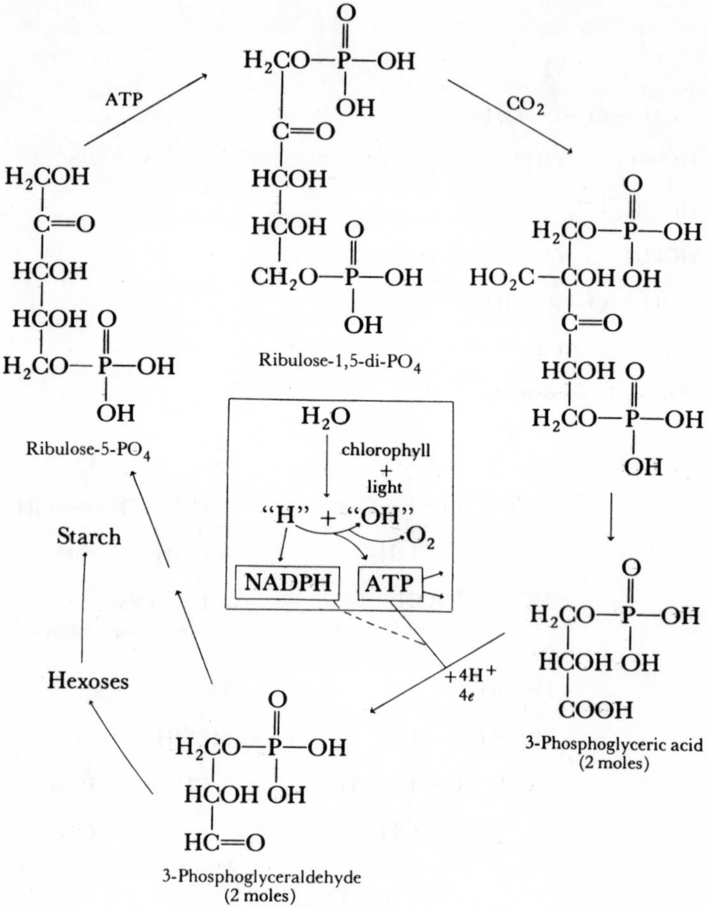

Fig. 5-4. Path of carbon in photosynthesis.

$$\left[\begin{array}{c} \quad\quad\quad \text{OH} \quad\quad\quad \text{OH} \\ \text{HO—P—OCH}_2\text{CHCOOH} \\ \quad\quad \| \\ \quad\quad \text{O} \end{array} \right]$$

3-Phosphoglyceric acid

It will be recalled that 3-phosphoglyceric acid is an intermediate in glycolysis. Thus, synthesis of carbohydrate can occur essentially by a reversal of glycolysis, beginning with phosphoglyceric acid. For clarity, the complete scheme is shown in Fig. 5-4. Examination of this scheme shows that to introduce a CO_2 molecule into triosephosphate requires three molecules of ATP and four reduction equivalents (four electrons).

The real point of photosynthesis seems not to be the fixation of carbon dioxide, but rather the use of light energy to produce ATP and reduce pyridine nucleotide (electrons). Photosynthesis uses for this process an important biological reductant, nicotinamide dinucleotide phosphate (NADPH).

Nicotinamide adenine diphosphate

Pyridine nucleotide is a derivative of the vitamin nicotinic acid (page 116) that transfers electrons.

Photosynthesis occurs in a particular part of the plant called the *chloroplast*. The chloroplast is similar in size to the mitochondrion and contains all the green coloring material of the plants, chlorophyll. We may regard chlorophyll as Nature's apparatus for converting light energy to chemical energy.

Arnon and his co-workers were able to isolate chloroplasts from plant cells. The chloroplasts carry out the following reaction:

$$NADP + ADP + CO_2 + chloroplasts + H_2O \rightarrow CH_2O + O_2$$

If CO_2 is removed the following partial reaction occurs:

$$Light + chloroplasts + NADP + ADP + H_2O \rightarrow$$
$$NADPH + ATP + O_2$$

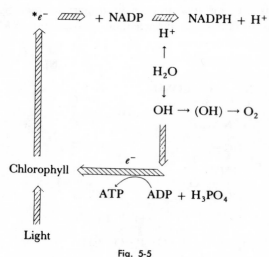

Fig. 5-5

$*e^-$ represents excited electron. The hatched arrows represent the path of the electron.

Addition of CO_2 permits completion of the reaction, that is, formation of (CH_2O).

Arnon next asked, how does light energy form ATP and NADPH? From physical chemistry we know that if an electron goes from a higher to a lower energy level, energy is released. Thus, if light can raise an electron to a higher level, all that is necessary is to capture the energy as it returns to its original state. This is illustrated in a scheme by Arnon (Fig. 5-5). Thus, the excited electron from chlorophyll eventually goes to a lower level resulting in energy conserved in the now familiar energy-rich phosphate bond.

Thus we see that a method evolved permitting the synthesis of carbohydrate (sucrose). This material provided a foodstuff for the animal kingdom. Animals that are wholly or partially vegetarians depend on the continuity of this important reaction. When we consider that carnivores in turn depend on the herbivorous animals for food, it is easy to appreciate how life depends either directly or indirectly upon the conversion of light energy to chemical energy. This process is illustrated in Fig. 5-6, where glucose is seen to enter such organs as liver or muscle after being generated in the intestine during the digestion of carbohydrates.

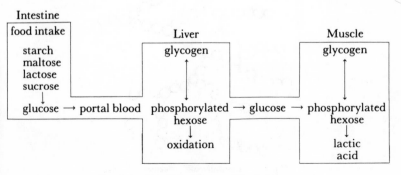

Fig. 5-6. Digestion and generation of glucose.

Glycogen Biosynthesis

The food that we consume, if it contains compounds that can be degraded to smaller sugars, is converted to the hexose sugar, glucose. Then, by means of the portal blood, this sugar is carried to the liver where it is converted to phosphorylated glucose. In the previous chapter we discussed the oxidation of this phosphorylated glucose to carbon dioxide and water. Like so many compounds occurring in living organisms, glucose may be used by several systems, depending on the demand. The prime force behind the oxidation is a demand for energy for various chemical and mechanical processes.

Sometimes our supply of phosphorylated hexoses is greater than the demand; then we have a surplus. This surplus may be stored in a readily utilizable form, glycogen

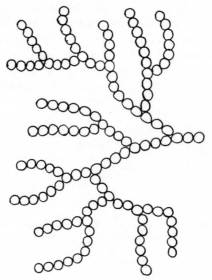

Fig. 5-7. Diagrammatic structure of glycogen. Each circle represents a glucose molecule.

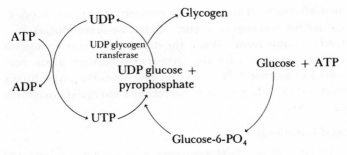

Fig. 5-8. Glycogen synthesis.

(animal starch). In a way this system is analogous to laws of supply and demand: home-grown tomatoes, for instance, that cannot be eaten during the harvest season are often canned by the family quartermaster, to be used at a later date. In effect we "can" glucose as glycogen. Glycogen is a large molecule consisting of many glucose units (Fig. 5-7).

Let us now examine how glycogen is made. Fig. 5-8 illustrates this process. The phosphorylated glucose is glucose-6-PO_4. This substance is formed by a kinase (that is, an enzyme that attaches a phosphate to a sugar molecule, using ATP). Glucose-6-PO_4 is then converted to glucose-1-phosphate by an enzyme which transfers the phosphate from one carbon to another. In essence we transfer the phosphate on the number 6 carbon to carbon 1 via a coenzyme (another form of catalyst; part of an enzyme system) called glucose-1,6-diphosphate. This is illustrated in Fig. 5-9. The glucose-1-PO_4 that is formed then combines with another coenzyme, uridine triphosphate, forming uridine diphosphoglucose. This coenzyme then transfers the glucose to a "primer" to

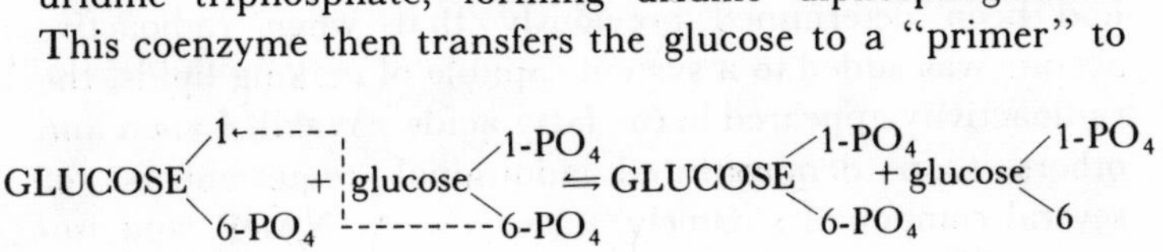

$$\text{GLUCOSE}\begin{array}{c} 1\text{-----} \\ \diagdown \\ 6\text{-}PO_4 \end{array} + \begin{array}{c} \text{glucose} \\ \text{-------} \\ 6\text{-}PO_4 \end{array}\begin{array}{c} 1\text{-}PO_4 \\ \diagup \end{array} \rightleftharpoons \text{GLUCOSE}\begin{array}{c} 1\text{-}PO_4 \\ \diagup \\ \diagdown \\ 6\text{-}PO_4 \end{array} + \text{glucose}\begin{array}{c} 1\text{-}PO_4 \\ \diagup \\ \diagdown \\ 6 \end{array}$$

Fig. 5-9

form glycogen. This primer, a polymer of glucose, is essential for the reaction to occur. Thus, we store glucose in a readily usable form. When the demand is great enough, it is a simple matter for the glycogen to be once again converted to glucose-1-PO_4, then to glucose-6-PO_4, and finally oxidized to carbon dioxide, water, and energy via oxidation pathways.

Lipid Biosynthesis

Investigations of fat synthesis were recently stimulated when it was shown that excess lipids may play a role in various heart disorders, particularly those diseases involving a deposition of cholesterol (Chapter 1) in the blood vessels. Such a deposit results in an impaired blood circulation which finally becomes so extensive that heart failure occurs. Thus, the importance of learning how lipids are synthesized and how the process is controlled is obvious.

After elucidation of the mechanism of fatty acid catabolism by β-oxidation (the two-carbon "scissoring" process referred to in Chapter 3), it was assumed that fat synthesis may occur by a reversal of these processes. It will be recalled that oxidation of fats occurred in the mitochondria. The theory that such a reversal might account for synthesis was soon refuted when it was shown that biosynthesis occurred in the nonmitochondrial fraction, specifically in the soluble components of the cell.

As with many biochemical processes, once the intracellular location and the required reactants were known, elucidation of the mechanism occurred with rapidity. It had been determined previously that when radioactive acetate was added to a system capable of making lipids, the radioactivity appeared in the fatty acids. Wakil, Lynen and others soon demonstrated additional requirements for several compounds, namely, coenzyme A, NADP, and isocitrate. The need for coenzyme A suggested the role of acetyl coenzyme A, since fatty acid synthesis is an endergonic (energy-requiring) reductive process; the requirement for NADP was hypothesized to furnish hydrogen (in the form of NADPH). The reductant might in turn be pictured as isocitrate, mediated by isocitric dehydrogenase, which is known to catalyze two of the Krebs cycle reactions.

$$\text{Isocitrate} + \text{NADP} \rightarrow \text{NADPH} + \text{H}^+ + \text{CO}_2 + \alpha\text{-ketoglutarate}$$

(Krebs cycle reactions 4, 5, Fig. 3-2.)

However, if NADPH was substituted for isocitrate, fatty acid synthesis did not occur. What then was the role of isocitrate? Since one of the products was carbon dioxide, the researchers tried substituting carbon dioxide for isocitrate. Fortunately, this move succeeded, and fatty acid synthesis was shown to occur in the presence of acetate, coenzyme A, NADPH, and carbon dioxide. Next, radioactive carbon dioxide was used to ascertain whether this radioactivity became part of the fatty acids. Another dilemma appeared when it was found that none of this label appeared in the fatty acids that were formed. Yet carbon dioxide was required!

It was hypothesized that possibly carbon dioxide combined in some way with acetyl coenzyme A to form an intermediate complex. The fact that this supposition was true was shown when the CoA derivative of malonic acid [the next larger compound beyond acetate, a diacid having three carbon atoms ($HOOCCH_2COOH$)], was isolated as a product of the reaction

$$CH_3\overset{\displaystyle O}{\underset{\displaystyle \|}{C}}S{-}CoA + C^{14}O_2 \rightarrow HO\overset{\displaystyle O}{\underset{\displaystyle \|}{C}}{}^{14}\underset{\underset{\displaystyle H_2}{|}}{C}{-}\overset{\displaystyle O}{\underset{\displaystyle \|}{C}}S{-}CoA$$

Also, if acetyl coenzyme A and carbon dioxide were replaced with malonyl coenzyme A, long-chain fatty acids were synthesized in the absence of a separate requirement for carbon dioxide. Malonyl CoA thus appeared to be the only necessary precursor of fatty acids, in the presence of the appropriate enzymes.

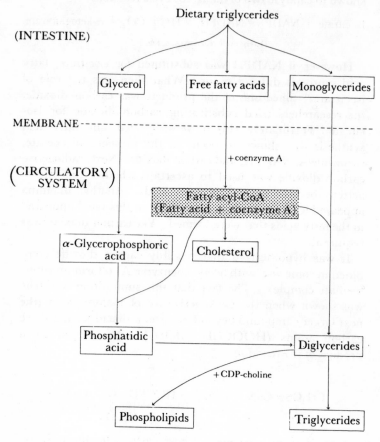

Fig. 5-10. Synthesis of tissue lipids.

So far as the total lipid picture is concerned, this is only part of the story, since in nature the lipids exist as parts of other chemical compounds. Besides fatty acids and fats, other lipids include phospholipids (these contain a nitrogenous base, glycerol, phosphate, and fatty acids); also cholesterol and related sterols.

The normal diet contains ample (often excessive) amounts of lipid precursors. These are usually triglycerides and the relation of these constituents in our food to complex lipids is shown in Fig. 5-10. The triglycerides do not enter as such

$$
\begin{array}{c}
\begin{array}{l}
\quad\quad\quad\ \ \overset{O}{\overset{\|}{}} \\
CH_2OC(CH_2)_nCH_3 \\
\quad\quad\ \ \overset{O}{\overset{\|}{}} \\
HCOC(CH_2)_nCH_3 \\
\quad\quad\ \ \overset{O}{\overset{\|}{}} \\
CH_2O\!-\!P\!-\!OH \\
\quad\quad\quad\ | \\
\quad\quad\quad OH
\end{array}
\quad + \quad
\left[HOCH_2CH_2\overset{+}{N}(CH_3)_3 \right] OH^- \longrightarrow
\end{array}
$$

Phosphatidic acid   Choline

$$
H_2O \ + \ \left[
\begin{array}{l}
\quad\quad\quad\ \ \overset{O}{\overset{\|}{}} \\
CH_2OC(CH_2)_nCH_3 \\
\quad\quad\ \ \overset{O}{\overset{\|}{}} \\
HCOC(CH_2)_nCH_3 \\
\quad\quad\quad\quad\ \ \overset{O}{\overset{\|}{}} \\
CH_2O\!-\!P\!-\!O\!-\!CH_2CH_2\overset{+}{N}(CH_3)_3 \\
\quad\quad\quad\ | \\
\quad\quad\quad OH
\end{array}
\right] OH^-
$$

Lecithin

$$\begin{array}{ccc}
\underset{\text{Phosphatidic acid}}{
\begin{array}{l}
\overset{\overset{\displaystyle O}{\|}}{CH_2OC}(CH_2)_nCH_3 \\
\overset{\overset{\displaystyle O}{\|}}{HCOC}(CH_2)_nCH_3 \\
\overset{\overset{\displaystyle O}{\|}}{CH_2O-P-OH} \\
OH
\end{array}}
& \longrightarrow &
\underset{\text{Diglyceride}}{
\begin{array}{l}
\overset{\overset{\displaystyle O}{\|}}{CH_2OC}(CH_2)_nCH_3 \\
\overset{\overset{\displaystyle O}{\|}}{HCOC}(CH_2)_nCH_3 \\
CH_2OH
\end{array}}
\end{array}$$

into a cell containing the machinery to manufacture complex lipids, but are first converted to glycerol, fatty acids, or monoglycerides. Once the glycerol enters a cell capable of making lipids, it may be converted to α-glycerophosphoric acid. Combination of α-glycerophosphoric acid with two fatty acids results in the synthesis of phosphatidic acid. Quick examination suggests that all that is necessary to form a lipid such as lecithin (phosphatidyl choline) is to add choline; *but*, as often is true in biological systems, this direct conversion does not occur. Rather the phosphatidic acid is converted to a diglyceride.

The other constituents of lecithin, namely choline and phosphate, are combined with another coenzyme, cytidine triphosphate (CTP), to yield cytidine diphosphocholine (CDP-choline). (Cytidine is a nucleoside, derived from one of the bases found in nucleic acids (Chapter 1). It also

$$\left[(CH_3)_3 \overset{+}{N} CH_2CH_2O - \overset{\overset{\displaystyle O}{\|}}{\underset{\underset{\displaystyle OH}{|}}{P}} - O - \overset{\overset{\displaystyle O}{\|}}{\underset{\underset{\displaystyle OH}{|}}{P}} - O\text{-Cytidine} \right] OH^-$$

CDP-choline

occurs free in living cells.) Next the CDP-choline reacts with the diglyceride, resulting in the synthesis of lecithin. This reaction scheme is typical of those involved in phospholipid biosynthesis.

One of the modern pictures of biochemistry evolved when Bloch and his colleagues completed the story of cholesterol biosynthesis. Although they demonstrated the way in which this particular compound was made in the biological system, this also introduced the means by which many other sterols

$$\left[\text{cytidine-O}-\overset{\overset{\displaystyle O}{\|}}{\underset{\underset{\displaystyle OH}{|}}{P}}-O-\overset{\overset{\displaystyle O}{\|}}{\underset{\underset{\displaystyle OH}{|}}{P}}-OCH_2CH_2\overset{+}{N}(CH_3)_3 \right] OH^-$$

$$+$$

$$\begin{array}{c} \overset{\overset{\displaystyle O}{\|}}{CH_2OC(CH_2)_nCH_3} \\ | \quad \overset{\displaystyle O}{\|} \\ H\overset{|}{C}OC(CH_2)_nCH_3 \\ | \\ CH_2OH \end{array} \longrightarrow$$

Diglyceride

$$\text{cytidine-O}-\overset{\overset{\displaystyle O}{\|}}{\underset{\underset{\displaystyle OH}{|}}{P}}-OH \quad + \quad \left[\begin{array}{c} \overset{\overset{\displaystyle O}{\|}}{CH_2OC(CH_2)_nCH_3} \\ | \quad \overset{\displaystyle O}{\|} \\ H\overset{|}{C}OC(CH_2)_nCH_3 \\ | \quad \overset{\displaystyle O}{\|} \\ CH_2O-P-O(CH_2)_2\overset{+}{N}(CH_3)_3 \end{array} \right] OH^-$$

Cytidine monophosphate   Lecithin

may be made. Using radioactive acetate they showed that all of the carbon atoms in cholesterol arose from the carbon atoms of acetate. (To illustrate the process involved, we may label the carbons of acetate as *m* for methyl and *c* for carbonyl

$$\underset{m}{CH_3}\underset{c}{COOH.})$$

Using two different radioactive compounds, they were able to show which carbon atoms of cholesterol derived from *m* and which from *c*. Such a procedure is analagous to marking the *m* as a red carbon and the *c* as a green carbon. Then the cholesterol can be isolated and the color of the carbons in cholesterol determined. Unfortunately, because the carbon atoms of acetate cannot be colored red or green, two experiments were needed. In one experiment, *m* was labeled with C^{14} and the cholesterol was isolated. It was found that all of the carbon atoms in cholesterol arising from *m* were radioactive, whereas those from *c* were unlabeled. In a similar manner, in a second experiment the *c* was labeled with C^{14} and the cholesterol was isolated. Then the labeling pattern was reversed—the carbon atoms arising from *c* were radioactive and those from *m* were not. If we represent *m* by ○ and *c* by ●, the location of these carbons in cholesterol is:

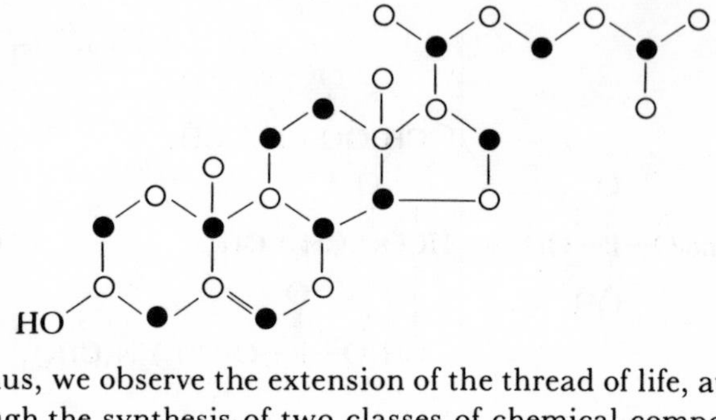

Thus, we observe the extension of the thread of life, at first through the synthesis of two classes of chemical compounds

—carbohydrates and lipids. These are incorporated, along with proteins, into a fabric that becomes the whole organism, in a manner that is largely under genetic control, modified in certain circumstances by specific hormones and vitamins that may constitute parts of specific enzyme systems. The "stuff" of proteins and nucleic acids has already been discussed; the reader is referred to the selected readings for the means by which the nucleic acids are synthesized.

We are here concerned not only with the indefinite replication of individual compounds but also with the synthesis of the whole organism. This phenomenon, whereby the entire creature develops from a single cell, is a fascinating

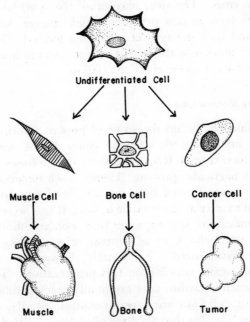

Fig. 5-11. Differentiation and growth.

study for the scientist who is interested in growth and differentiation (Fig. 5-11). By growth, we mean the increase in size or numbers of the same kind of cell, whereas differentiation implies the creation of a new cell-type that in turn leads to the production of the latter's own progeny. Not only is this change self-perpetuating, it is generally irreversible. The original cell contains the potential to become many kinds of cells; the expression of this potential leads to new types or to differentiation. Usually these changes follow definite genetic patterns. However, occasionally something goes awry and the cell in question may be converted to a cancer cell; this type of change might also be termed one sort of differentiation. A chemical agent in cancer formation may be a virus. The virus may cause the synthesis of new chemicals such as new proteins, which change the protein pattern and thus the type of cell being formed. Thus, we appreciate more fully the importance of learning much more about the basic process of differentiation.

Regulatory Mechanisms

It is plausible within the scope of present information to construct an hypothesis whereby genes (DNA molecules) convey information to RNA, and there then follows the synthesis of a particular protein. Thence, each molecular generation is characterized by the synthesis of new molecules fabricated exactly as those made before. If this were to continue ad infinitum, it is apparent that soon an infinite number of a particular kind of protein or expanding organs would be synthesized. Fortunately, biosynthetic control mechanisms exist which limit this proliferation. The very fact that each organism does essentially reach a finite mass rather than an infinite one suggests control. Studies of these control mechanisms thus far have often been limited to unicellular organisms such as bacteria, but an extrapolation of these mechanisms may be partially correct for multicellular organisms.

The necessity for regulatory mechanisms is illustrated in an example given by Bernard Davis. Let us examine what happens if a bacterium Z grows 1% faster than bacterium Y. If 10 cells each of Z and Y are inoculated into a flask, overnight they may complete 30 generations. In 30 generations, the ratio of Z/Y would be 1.35 and eventually Z would completely outgrow Y.

Often this control mechanism has been called "feedback" thus relating it to concepts in communications engineering. The implication in feedback is that some product of an anabolic pathway somehow returns information to tell something (an enzyme) to halt production of a certain chemical. Thus, let us view a certain anabolic (or biosynthetic) pathway as:

$$A \underset{E_a}{\rightarrow} B \underset{E_b}{\rightarrow} C \underset{E_c}{\rightarrow} D$$

(E_a, E_b, E_c refer to enzymes converting A to B, B to C, and C to D, respectively). When a certain amount of D is synthesized, it then becomes an inhibitor of the total pathway. This may be accomplished by affecting the action of an enzyme such as E_a, as shown in Fig. 5-12. This is called "feedback inhibition"; that is, the action of the enzyme is inhibited and the result is the stopping of conversion of A to B. Another possibility exists and this is an inhibition of the *synthesis* of enzyme (E_a). This is called "repression." We may expand our scheme as shown in Fig. 5-13. Limiting the synthesis of E_a would eventually have an effect identical to feedback inhibition, that is, decreased manufacture of B and, of course,

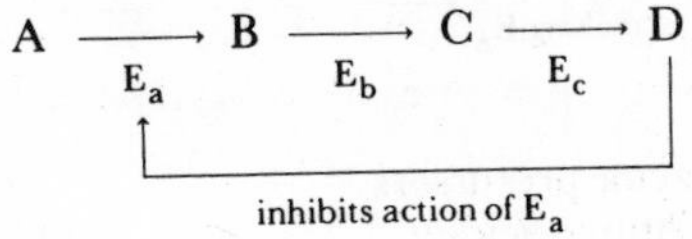

$$A \xrightarrow[E_a]{} B \xrightarrow[E_b]{} C \xrightarrow[E_c]{} D$$

inhibits action of E_a

Fig. 5-12

eventually C and D. Both of these ideas are examples of a feedback mechanism.

Since our particular enzyme (E_a), like many enzymes, is specific in that it will react only with A, the implication is that there is also something inherent in A that will permit it to react only with E_a. This is necessary for the following considerations. Often in biochemical systems a certain compound may be an intermediate in the synthesis of more than one compound. In our example suppose that A is such an intermediate that may be converted to D or another compound (Fig. 5-14). To carry out the functions of a particular cell it may be that a finite amount of either or both D and G are required. The orderly development and function of this cell requires some means by which the correct amounts of D or G are made. Feedback inhibition is one means by which this is accomplished. That is, when adequate amounts of the product D are manufactured, then an inhibition of E_a occurs with the result that A no longer is converted to D. Then, A can be converted to G and, carrying this further, when adequate amounts of G are synthesized, it in turn will specifically inhibit E_g. Thus we have two control mechanisms, as shown in Fig. 5-15. If D were not specific for E_a it could conceivably also inhibit E_e with the result that G would not be synthesized. If G were a compound essential to the life of the cell, the result would be death—certainly a fate not enjoyed by the organism.

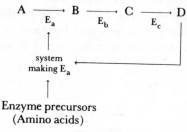

$$A \xrightarrow{E_a} B \xrightarrow{E_b} C \xrightarrow{E_c} D$$

system
making E_a

Enzyme precursors
(Amino acids)

Fig. 5-13

The other feedback mechanism was referred to as repression, that is, the inhibition of the synthesis of a particular enzyme. In our discussion of the synthesis of specific enzymes a procedure was mentioned whereby DNA passes information to RNA, which in turn modulates the placing together of certain amino acids in a particular sequence. Consideration of this process in itself suggests that when all the necessary components (or chemicals) are present, there is no reason not to suppose that the process continues indefinitely. This may be likened to a dam with its generators producing hydroelectric power. If we have infinite amounts of water, the only things that limit the amount of hydroelectric power that we can produce are the generators, that is, the equipment to convert water power into electric power. Our chemicals may here be likened to the water, that is, they are in abundance. The amount of power is limited to the number of generators, and the number of generators is in turn limited by the capacity to manufacture them. By analogy our enzymes are the generators and their numbers are limited by the systems making them. The manufacture of generators may, however, be limited not by the raw materials, but also by available labor force. Likewise, the manufacture of enzymes is influenced not only by the raw materials (amino acids) but by some other means analogous to the labor force. In the system

$$A \xrightarrow[E_a]{} B \xrightarrow[E_b]{} C \xrightarrow[E_c]{} D$$

the orderly development of a cell requires the making of correct amounts of E_a, E_b and E_c. A goal is to find the site of repression of the synthesis of each of these enzymes, preferably

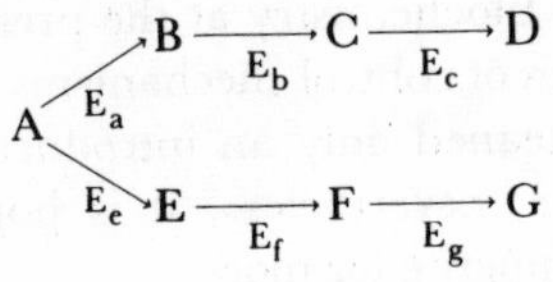

Fig. 5-14

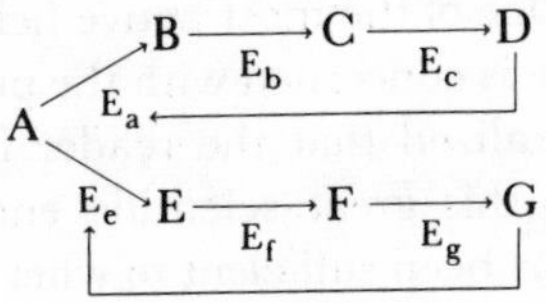

Fig. 5-15

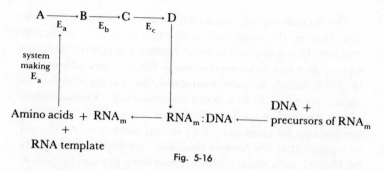

Fig. 5-16

in terms of a chemical entity. One such entity is messenger RNA (RNA_m). Messenger RNA is that RNA which controls the synthesis of a particular enzyme.

The feedback mechanism, repression, may act as a control mechanism as follows: the function of the repressor is to interfere with the synthesis of a particular enzyme, as is shown in Fig. 5-16. Thus, if D is the repressor, the suggestion is that in some way it interferes with the making of a messenger RNA (RNA_m) necessary for the synthesis of E_a. General models for this reaction have been prepared by Jacob and Monod and the reader is referred to those listed under selected readings.

Not only do cellular control mechanisms offer an orderly picture of the development of a particular organism, but also several medical implications are inherent in this portrait. The loss of a particular enzyme or lack of control of its synthesis may lead to an alteration, the result of which is disease. Cancer may be an example where control is lacking; a result is abnormal growth. This suggestion in itself emphasizes the necessity of understanding normal control.

One of the most active fields in biochemistry at the present time is concerned with the problem of control mechanisms. It is realized that the reader has gleaned only an introduction into this great scientific endeavor; nevertheless, it is hoped it has been sufficient to whet the appetite for more.

THE REMOTE BEGINNINGS:
SOME SPECULATIONS

MILLIONS of years ago, but yet long after the formation of those things we consider inanimate, an infinitesimal speck developed in the primeval oceans. This was a tenacious speck, that persevered, multiplied, and became alive. Man was not present to observe the beginnings of life; only much later did there emerge from this vast aqueous milieu the land rover. Although the details of this story may remain beyond our reach, our curiosities will never be satisfied until the day when man fully understands life's beginnings.

Perhaps even more wondrous is the apparently orderly control by which this development occurred. Only recently have we gained some insight into the origin and possible ways in which this unidirectional path is controlled. (It may appear to be egocentric to concern ourselves with the study of life's beginning and its evolution to the present state, yet the devotion of scientists to understand life then and now must seem far nobler than does preoccupation with creating means to destroy our existence.)

Evolution of life requires but two things: one, the creation of those chemical moieties we recognize as part of life; the other, the control of the synthesis of these moieties. One of the remarkable observations that we may make concerning life is that it began, and in an orderly fashion arrayed itself in such a manner that the right amounts of each chemical entity were put together resulting in complete organisms. Not only does this suggest the making of simple molecules from elements, but the formation of control mechanisms that regulate the amounts of molecules manufactured.

How did life begin? We can only approach an answer. Discarding metaphysical considerations, what model can we concoct that is based on scientific knowledge? One interesting exercise is to explore space with the hope of finding other living forms, perhaps much simpler, the likes of which might pose as possible progenitors of present-day species. Another is to attempt to create life in the test tube. Possibly we can only indulge in mental gymnastics; the chasm of the unfamiliar is immense. Yet lack of familiarity has never deterred scientists from searching into the unknown. In the field of biochemistry, curiosity about man has been a powerful stimulus behind research, not only to fit together observable parts, but to include speculations on life's origins.

The first assault is to surmise what the earth (or any other hospitable environment) may have been like when infinitesimal life began. It is presumed here that the origin of the infinitesimal was nothing; that is, that life developed from nonliving precursors. Development of a living supermolecule from nonliving precursors may have occurred many times, but we regard here as important the speck that persevered—that struggled, organized, grew, reproduced; that has somehow reached its present stage of continuing improvement; that is currently represented as man.

The origin of life may conveniently be divided into two parts: one, chemical evolution, as suggested by Calvin; the other, formation of systems. The only requirement for either of these to occur is to have the right conditions at the right time with the right material substances. At first glance it may seem expedient to call this impossible. On reflection, though, is it not true that this also describes the morphogenesis of living organisms today? Impossibility is a relative term— every event has a possibility, that is, a chance that it will occur. All that is required for the origin of a living organism is that a probable event occur *at least once*. Fortunately, time has been on our side. Orderly evolution since the origin of a living organism may suggest that it had to be unidirectional or fail.

Over the years both scientist and philosopher have offered theories based on everything from sound evidence to opiate dreams concerning the origin of life. Whether anything will ever be more than conjecture we cannot say, but possibly we can simplify terms to see what we need, as is done in Fig. 6-1. This simplification at least tells us what knowledge to seek: first, in the formation of the inorganic world, metals, oxides, silicates; then in the formation of simple organic compounds such as cyanide, methane, carbon dioxide, carbonates; eventually in the formation of organic acids, amino acids, purines, and pyrimidines; and finally in the formation of complex molecules such as proteins or nucleic acids.

At this point we come to the problem of defining life. A simple definition might be that life is a self-renewal of the chemical constituents of its substances. Since present information indicates a close connection and essential relation between nucleic acids and proteins, conceivably the primitive living organism might better be equated to the simpler viruses. The simplest example would be an organism with one gene (one DNA molecule?) that directs the synthesis of one protein. Then from the primitive living organism develops more complex systems, and our story becomes merely a restatement of Darwinian evolution. The scientist is interested in that part

TABLE 6-1. Possible Steps in the Formation of Solar Systems (Urey)[a]

Chronology and process occurring	Phases and objects	Chemical group	Temperature, °C
1. Solar dust cloud	Gas	H_2, inert gases, CH_4	$<< 0$
Formation of sun; discharge of gas and dust	Dust	Silicates, FeO, FeS, solid H_2O, NH_3	
2. Preprotoplanet; early protoplanet	Gas	H_2, inert gases, H_2O, NH_3, CH_4	0
Accumulation of planetesimals and substances of moon	Dust Planetesimals	Silicates, FeO, FeS	
		Silicates, FeO, FeS, hydrated minerals, NH_4Cl, solid H_2O, NH_3	
3. High-temperature stage. Reduction of FeO; loss of gases and volatilized silicates	Gas	H_2, inert gases, H_2O, N_2, CH_4, H_2S, volatilized silicates	
	Large planetesimals	FeO, hydrated minerals, FeS, NH_4Cl, metallic Fe, C, Fe_3C, Sn	2000
	Small planetesimals	Silicates, metallic Fe, C, Fe_3C, Sn	
4. First and second low-temperature stages.	Gas	Mostly lost. Small amts. H_2, H_2O, N_2, CH_4, H_2S, inert gases	0
Final accumulation of earth	Planetesimals	Same as 3	
5. Final stage. Earth and moon complete	Moon	Silicates, a little metallic iron	Space: 0
	Earth	45% metallic iron, 55% silicates	Earth: 900 going to present temp.
	Atmosphere	H_2O, CH_4, H_2, $N_2 \rightarrow NH_3$	

[a] Oparin, A. I., "The Origin of Life on Earth," 3rd ed., p. 138, Academic Press, Inc., 1957.

that extends from point X (simple organic molecules) in Fig. 6-1 through the primitive living organism.

Fortunately our understanding of the formation of the earth into a definitive real mass is aided by the constant formation of new solar systems, which we can study. The relations of the parameters involved are best illustrated by Urey (Table 6-1). At the inorganic stage in the earth's development, the atmosphere probably consisted of water, methane, hydrogen, oxygen, and ammonia. Thus, the compounds in a primitive

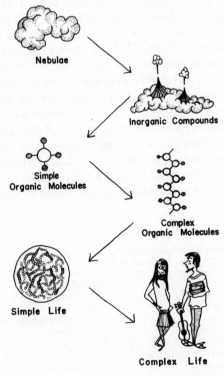

Nebulae

Inorganic Compounds

Simple Organic Molecules

Complex Organic Molecules

Simple Life

Complex Life

Fig. 6-1. Evolutionary theory of the origin of life.

TABLE 6-2.   Compounds Formed from Irradiation of C^{14}-labeled
Methane, Ammonia, Water, and HCN[a]

Adenine	Glycine
5-Aminoimadazolecarboxamide	α-Alanine
Lactic acid	Aspartic acid

[a] From Palm, C., and Calvin, M., *J. Am. Chem. Soc.* **84,** 2115 (1962).

organism could at the most contain only these elements.
(Moreover, the principal constituents of present, known, living
matter consist of chemicals made from atoms of hydrogen,
carbon, oxygen, and nitrogen; the building materials have
obviously been available.) Putting them together into various
chemical bonds requires energy; *fortunately* three kinds of
energy that were probably available in the beginning (radia-
tion, ultraviolet light, and lightning) are all amenable to
laboratory experimentation. It is possible to place such compounds as water, methane, hydrogen, and nitrogen in a mixture, expose them to one of these sources of energy, initiate a
reaction, and isolate the products. Such experiments have
been done. The results obtained by Calvin are shown in
Table 6-2 and those by Horowitz and Miller in Table 6-3.

TABLE 6-3.   Compounds Formed from Sparking a Mixture
of CH_4, NH_3, H_2O, and H_2[a]

Glycine	Aspartic acid
Glycolic acid	Glutamic acid
Sarcosine	Iminodiacetic acid
Alanine	Iminoacetic-propionic acid
Lactic acid	Formic acid
N-Methylalanine	Acetic acid
α-Aminobutyric acid	Urea
β-Alanine	N-Methylurea
Succinic acid	

[a] From Horowitz, N. H., and Miller, S. L., *Fortschr. der. Naturstoffe* (1962).

Many of these simple organic compounds we now recognize as parts of living systems. Next, we need to study the more complex molecules such as nucleic acids or proteins. Fox has provided information from experiments relative to the origin

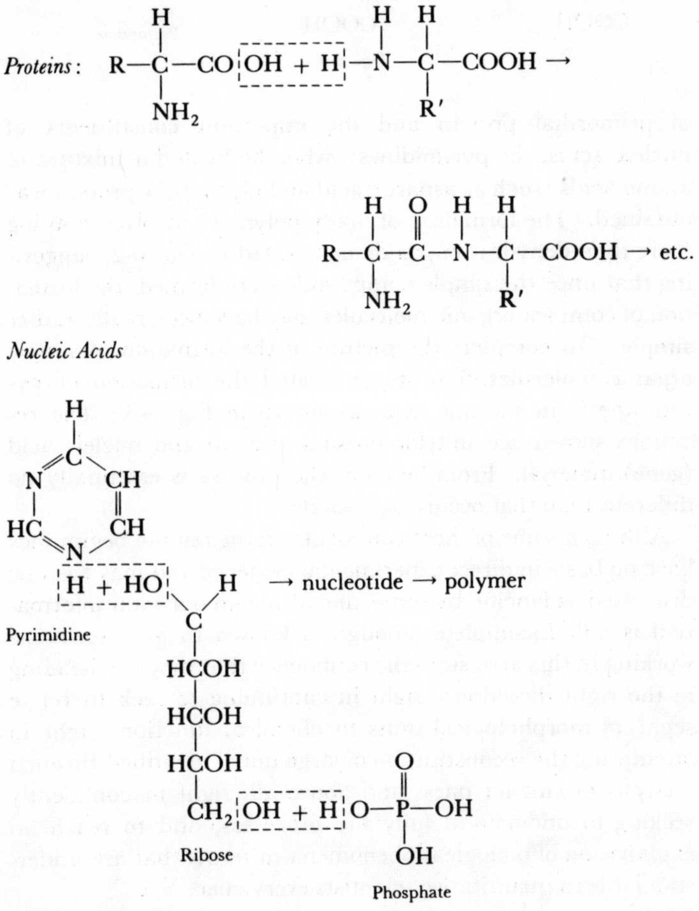

Fig. 6-2. Examples of elimination of water to form polymers from simple organic compounds.

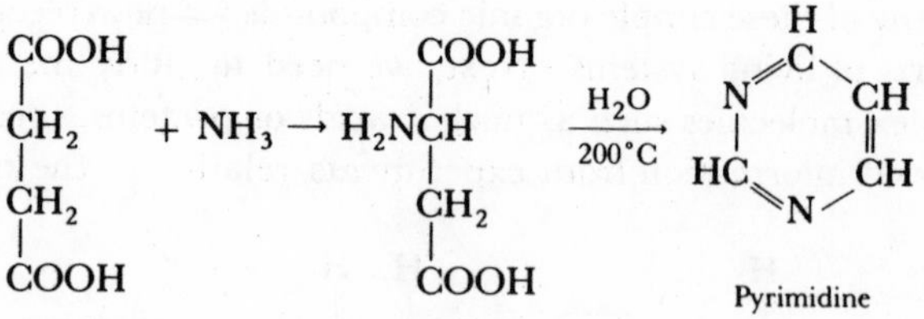

Fig. 6-3

of primordial protein and the important constituents of nucleic acids, the pyrimidines: when he heated a mixture of amino acids (such as aspartic acid and glycine), a protein was obtained. The formation of many polymers involves nothing more than dehydration, as demonstrated in Fig. 6-2, suggesting that once the simple compounds were formed, the formation of complex organic molecules may have been really rather simple. To complete the picture of the formation of simple organic molecules, Fox demonstrated the formation of pyrimidine from succinic acid, as shown in Fig. 6-3. The reactions shown account for possible protein and nucleic acid (gene) material. From here on, the process is essentially no different than that occurring each day.

Although some of these comments on the remote beginnings have no basis in direct experimental evidence and may even be dismissed as fanciful by some, and although our total information is still incomplete, enough is known to give scientists working in this area supreme confidence that they are heading in the right direction: right in continuing to seek to relate separate morphological units to chemical function; right in attempting the reconstitution of large units, identified through analysis of smaller ones; and above all, right in confidently seeking to understand fully life processes, and to reach an explanation of biological phenomena in terms that are understandable to quantitative scientists everywhere.

SELECTED READINGS

Chapter 1

Annual Review of Biochemistry. Annual Reviews, Inc., Palo Alto, Calif. (General.)

Chargaff, E., and Davidson, J. N., eds., "The Nucleic Acids," Vols. I–III, Academic Press, Inc., New York, 1955, 1960. (Nucleic acids.)

Fairley, J. L., and Kilgour, G. L., "Essentials of Biological Chemistry," Reinhold Publishing Corp., New York, 1963. (General.)

Fox, S. W., and Foster, J. F., "Introduction to Protein Chemistry," John Wiley and Sons, Inc., New York, 1957. (Proteins.)

Hanahan, D. J., "Lipids Chemistry," John Wiley and Sons, Inc., New York, 1960. (Lipids.)

Pigman, W., ed., "The Carbohydrates," Academic Press, Inc., New York, 1957. (Carbohydrates.)

Sebrell, W. H., Jr., and Harris, R. S., "The Vitamins," Academic Press, Inc., New York, 1954. (Vitamins.)

Chapter 2

Avery, O. T., MacLeod, C. M., and McCarty, M., "Studies on the Chemical Nature of the Substance Inducing Transformation of Pneumococcal Types," *J. Exptl. Med.* **79**, 137–158 (1944).

Cold Spring Harbor Symposium on Quantitative Biology, Long Island Biological Assoc., Cold Spring Harbor, N. Y., Vol. 26, 1962

Hoagland, M. B., "The Relationship of Nucleic Acid and Protein Synthesis as Revealed by Studies in Cell-free Systems," in Chargaff, E., and Davidson, J. N., "The Nucleic Acids," Vol. III, ch. 37, Academic Press, New York, 1960.

Potter, Van, "Nucleic Acid Outlines," Vol. I, Burgess Publishing Co., Minneapolis, 1960.

Proceedings of the 11th Annual Reunion of the Société de Chemie Physique, "Deoxyribonucleic Acid," Pergamon, New York, 1961.

Chapter 3

Cheldelin, V. H., "Metabolic Pathways in Microorganisms," John Wiley and Sons, New York, 1961.

Green, D. E., and Fleischer, S., "Mitochondrial Systems of Enzymes," in D. Greenberg, ed., "Metabolic Pathways," Vol. I, Academic Press, New York, 1960.

Klotz, I. M., "Some Principles of Energetics in Biochemical Reactions," Academic Press, New York, 1957.

Pardee, A. B., and Ingraham, L. L., "Free Energy and Entropy in Metabolism," in D. Greenberg, ed., "Metabolic Pathways." Vol. I, Academic Press, New York, 1960.

Chapter 4

Brachet, J., and Mirsky, A., eds., "The Cell," Vols. I–III, Academic Press, New York, 1955, 1960.

Chapter 5

Block, K., ed., "Lipid Metabolism," John Wiley and Sons, New York, 1960.

Hassid, W. F., "Biosynthesis of Complex Saccharides," in D. M. Greenberg, ed., "Metabolic Pathways," Vol. I, Academic Press, New York, 1960.

Jacob, and Monod, F., Cold Spring Harbor Symp. on Quant. Biol., Vol. 26, 1962.

Chapter 6

Anfinsen, C., "The Molecular Basis of Evolution," John Wiley and Sons, New York, 1959.

Oparin, A. I., "The Origin of Life on the Earth," 3rd ed., Academic Press, Inc., New York, 1957.

Oparin, A. I., "The Origin of Life," (Trans. by Serguis Morgulis), Dover Publications, Inc., New York, 1953.

APPENDIX

A. AMINO ACIDS COMMONLY OCCURRING IN PROTEINS

Monoamino Monocarboxylic Acids

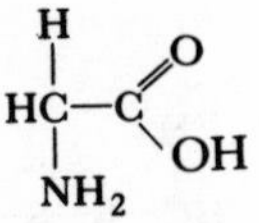

Glycine
(Aminoacetic acid)

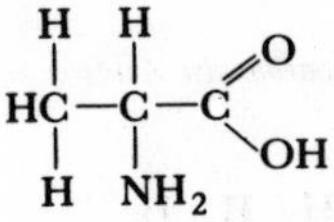

L(+)-Alanine
(α-Aminopropionic acid)

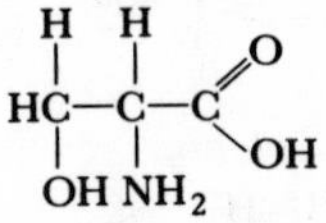

L(−)-Serine
(α-Amino-β-hydroxypropionic acid)

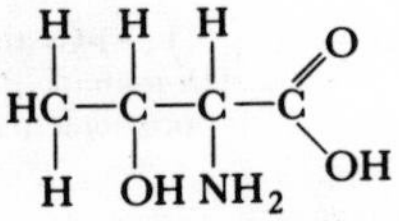

L(−)-Threonine
(α-Amino-β-hydroxybutyric acid)

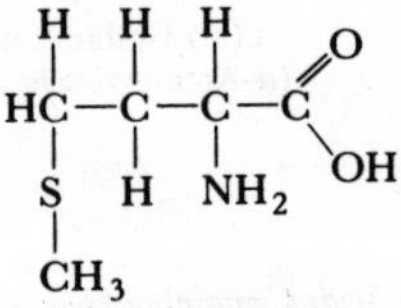

L(−)-Methionine
(α-Amino-γ-(methylmercapto)-butyric acid)

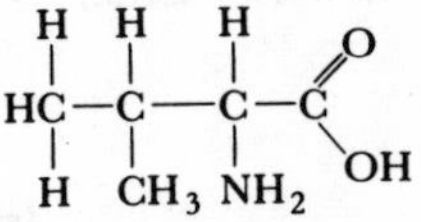

L(+)-Valine
(α-Aminoisovaleric acid)

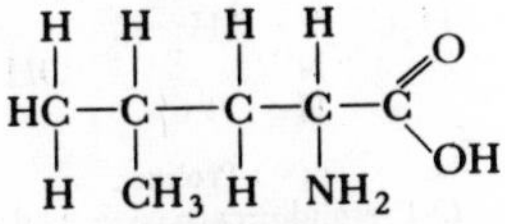

L(−)-Leucine
(α-Aminoisocaproic acid)

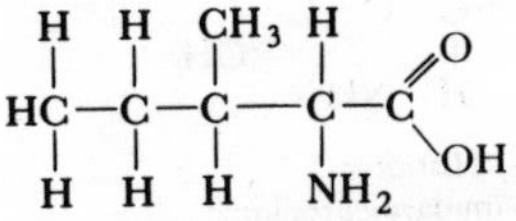

L(+)-Isoleucine
(α-Amino-β-methylvaleric acid)

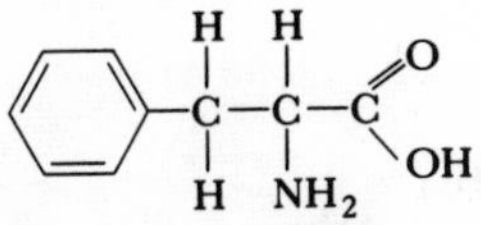

L(−)-Phenylalanine
(α-Amino-β-phenylpropionic acid)

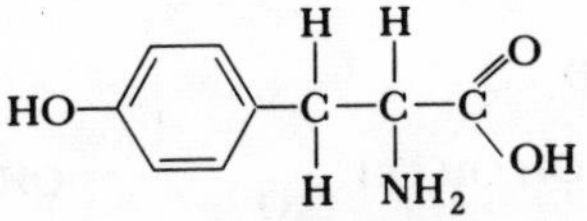

L(−)-Tyrosine
(α-Amino-β-(p-hydroxyphenyl)propionic acid)

113

Diamino Monocarboxylic Acids

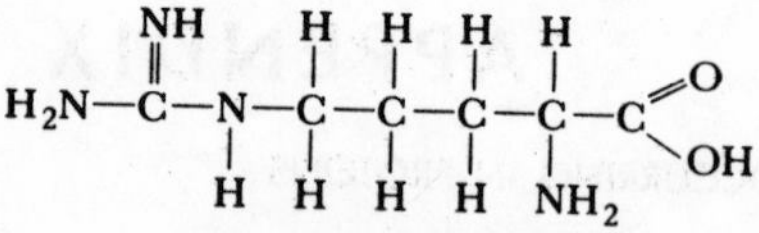

L(+)-Arginine
(α-Amino-δ-guanidinevaleric
acid)

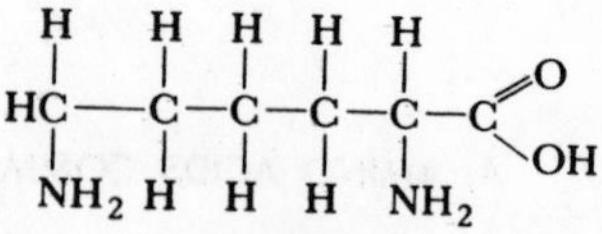

L(+)-Lysine
(α,ε-Diaminocaproic acid)

Amino Dicarboxylic Acids

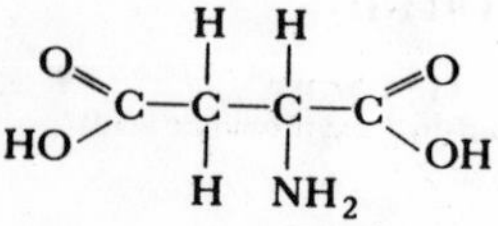

L(−)-Aspartic acid
(Aminosuccinic acid)

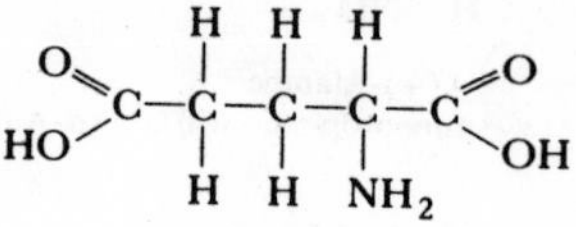

L(+)-Glutamic acid
(α-Aminoglutaric acid)

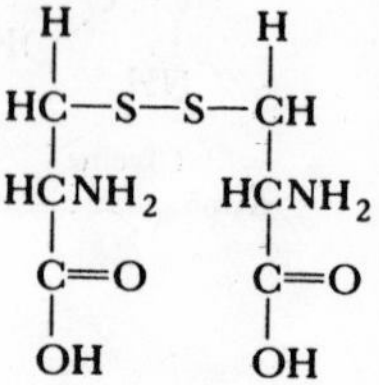

L(−)-Cystine
(Di-α-amino-β-thio-
propionic acid)

Amino Acids Containing Heterocyclic Rings

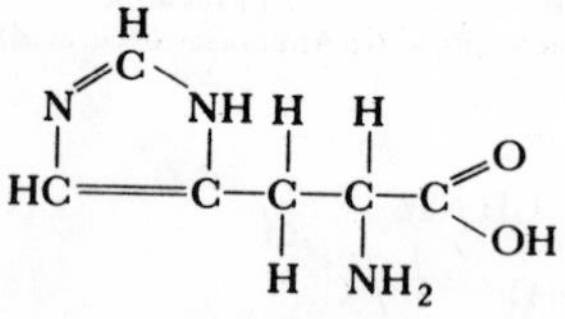

L(−)-Histidine
(α-Amino-β-imidazolepropionic
acid)

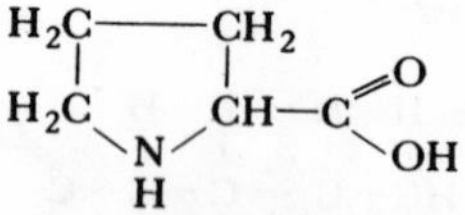

L(−)-Proline
(2-Pyrrolidinecarboxylic acid)

B.   CONSTITUENTS OF NUCLEIC ACIDS

Sugars

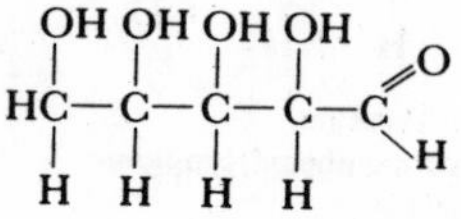

Ribose

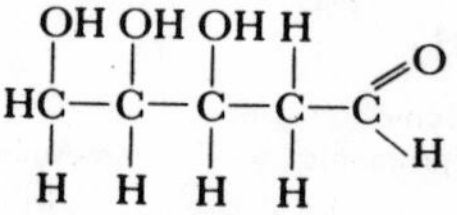

2-Deoxyribose

Nitrogenous Bases

Purines

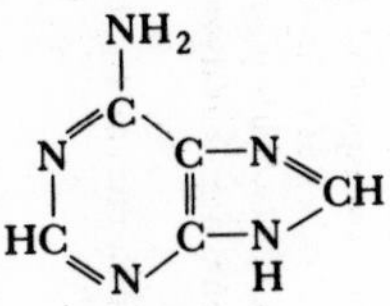

Adenine

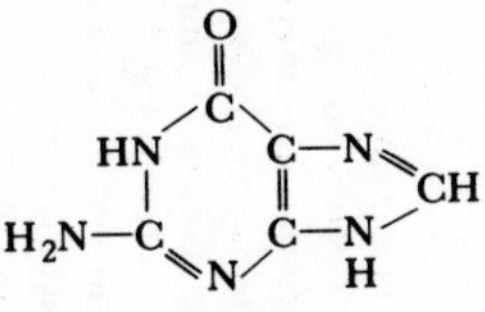

Guanine

Pyrimidines

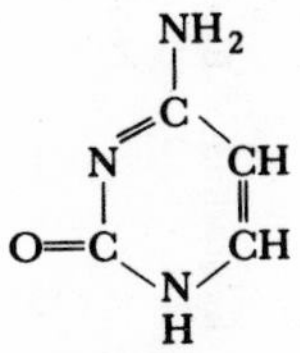

Cytosine

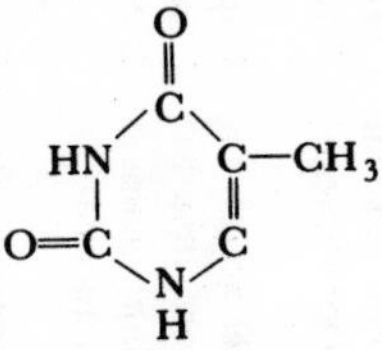

Thymine

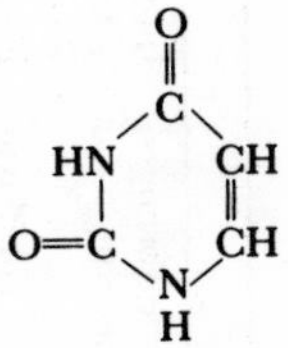

Uracil

Nucleoside

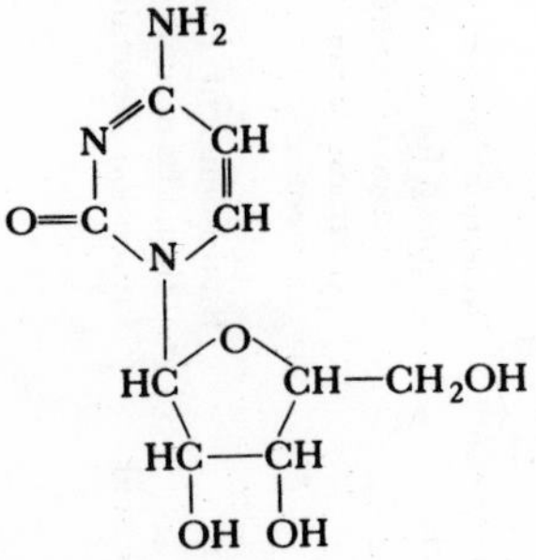

Cytosine riboside

Nucleotide

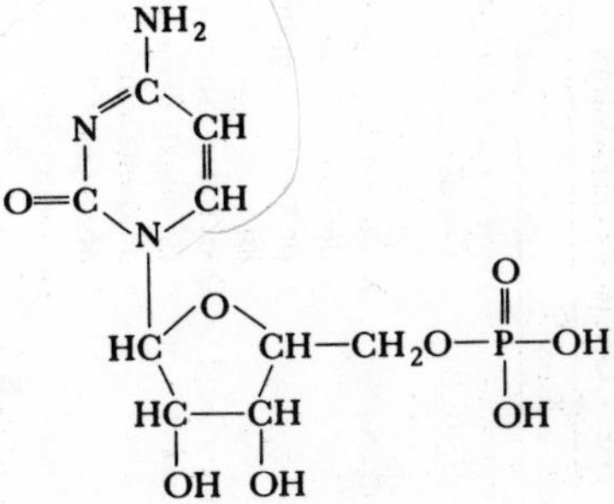

Cytosine ribotide

C. THE COMMON VITAMINS

Vitamin Name	Physiological function	Biochemical role
Thiamine (vitamin B_1)	Prevents beriberi; deficiency causes muscle soreness, loss of reflexes, enlargement of heart, neuritis	Integral part of enzyme that decarboxylates certain carboxylic acids; catalyzes oxidation of pyruvate, reactions of the pentose cycle (see Chapter 3)
Riboflavin	Required for normal rat growth; frank riboflavin deficiency poorly defined in humans, although it probably complicates beriberi, pellagra, kwashiorkor	Part of enzymes transporting electrons (see Chapter 3)
Nicotinic acid (niacin)	Deficiency causes pellagra in humans, blacktongue in dogs; dementia, dermatitis, anemia. Small amounts synthesized in body from dietary tryptophan (see Chapter 3)[a]	Constituent part of enzymes that transport electrons (Chapter 3); electrons are often transferred from nicotinic acid-containing enzymes to riboflavin-containing proteins (see above entry)
Pyridoxal (vitamin B_6)	Deficiency in rats causes growth failure, acrodynia (dermatitis, scaliness of skin on tail, ears, mouth). Deficiency may also produce morning sickness during pregnancy, vomiting in infants; anemia	Important for metabolism of amino acids; enzymes containing this vitamin catalyze transfer of the amino groups to certain keto acids (transamination); decarboxylation of amino acids, some synthesis of C—C bonds.
Pantothenic acid	Nutritional role in humans not yet determined. Required for growth, hair coloring in rats, proper function of adrenal glands. Deficiency may cause dizziness, other malfunctions of central nervous system	Enzymes containing this catalyst are needed for mobilization and transport of the acetyl ($-\overset{\overset{\displaystyle O}{\|}}{C}-CH_3$) group and other acyls in the Krebs cycle and in metabolism of fatty acids (Chapter 3)
Biotin	Biotin-deficient rats display muscular incoordination, loss of hair, dermatitis	Biotin-deficient enzymes catalyze CO_2 fixation in animal tissues
Folic acid	Prevention of certain types of anemia	Folic acid-containing enzymes catalyze mobilization and transfer of formyl group ($-\overset{\overset{\displaystyle O}{\|}}{C}-H$)

Vitamin	Deficiency / dietary role	Physiological function
Vitamin B$_{12}$ (cyanocobalamin)	Prevention of pernicious anemia	B$_{12}$-enzymes catalyze transfer of methyl (—CH$_3$) groups. These enzymes may accept formyl groups from folic acid enzymes, reduce them to methyl
Inositol	Unknown; reported to be required in diet of rats, mice, swine, poultry.	Catalytic role uncertain. This compound occurs as a structural component of certain phospholipids.
Choline	Like inositol, this is a vitamin of doubtful status; it appears unnecessary in diet when protein intake is adequate. When choline is needed, it appears to prevent deposition of excess fat in liver	Functions as part of biological methyl group transfer systems
Ascorbic acid (vitamin C)	Prevents scurvy, capillary fragility. Needed in diet by humans, other primates, guinea pigs	Uncertain; probably participates in biological oxidation-reduction, may be a biological "scavenger" that is easily oxidized, preventing oxidation of other essential metabolites.
Vitamin A	Prevents night blindness; deficiency causes keratinization (hardening) of epithelial cells. Growth failure in young individuals results.	Vitamin occurs in the eye as part of a protein that is a light-sensitive pigment. It is reversibly oxidized and reduced, being alternately bleached by light and regenerated in the dark. In vitamin A deficiency this protein ("visual purple") is nearly permanently bleached
Calciferol (vitamin D$_2$)	Prevents rickets in children, growing animals.	Uncertain. (This vitamin is regularly formed to some extent in the tissues, by ultraviolet irradiation of appropriate precursors in the skin).
Vitamin E (α-tocopherol)	Prevents sterility, muscular dystrophy	Uncertain; may be a biological "antioxidant" similiar to vitamin C (see above)
Vitamin K$_1$	Antihemorrhagic vitamin	Believed to participate as a catalyst in the synthesis within the liver of prothrombin, a blood-clotting protein

a Cornmeal is low in both tryptophan and niacin (see discussion on p. 15). For this reason cornmeal is often considered to be pellagragenic unless balanced by other more nutritious foodstuffs.

INDEX